The Periodic Table Series

Periodically, we're all geeks about the things we love and the Periodic Table Series has been created to celebrate this universal fact.

Inspired by The Periodic Table of Chemical Elements*, our experts have applied scientific logic to an eclectic range of subjects that regularly baffle beginners and fire-up fans. The outcome of this experiment is the essential guide you hold in your hand.

Geeky? Absolutely.
Hugely satisfying? Categorically.

*The Periodic Table of Chemical Elements orders all the known matter that makes up our world, from hydrogen to helium, by chemical properties and behaviour to give scientists a handy overview of a rather complex subject.

THE PERIODIC TABLE OF
CRICKET

JOHN STERN

EBURY
PRESS

10 9 8 7 6 5 4 3 2 1

Ebury Press, an imprint of Ebury Publishing,
20 Vauxhall Bridge Road,
London, SW1V 2SA

Ebury Press is part of the Penguin Random House
group of companies whose addresses can be found
at global.penguinrandomhouse.com

Copyright © Ebury Press 2016
Illustrations © Dave Will Design 2016

First published by Ebury Press in 2016

www.eburypublishing.co.uk

A CIP catalogue record for this book is available
from the British Library

ISBN: 9781785031823

Printed and bound in China by Toppen Leefung

Penguin Random House is committed to a
sustainable future for our business, our readers
and our planet. This book is made from Forest
Stewardship Council® certified paper.

Contents

The Periodic Table of
CRICKET

DEFENDERS & PRAGMATISTS   STYLISTS & ENTERTAINERS

1 E **H** Hobbs		**25** A **Tr** Trumper		**42** E **Fr** Fry
2 E **Hu** Hutton		**26** SA **Rb** B. Richards	**34** NZ **Cw** Crowe	**43** SA **Dv** de Villiers
3 E **By** Boycott	**18** E **Rh** Rhodes	**27** NZ **Mc** McCullum	**35** I **T** Tendulkar	**44** A **Ml** Miller
4 E **Gc** Gooch	**19** E **Lk** Laker	**28** E **Hm** Hammond	**36** WI **Lr** Lara	**45** P **Im** Imran
5 E **Ck** Cook / **10** E **Ba** Barrington	**20** WI **Gb** Gibbs	**29** E **Cm** Compton	**37** A **Wm** M. Waugh	**46** I **Kd** Kapil Dev
6 P **Ha** Hanif / **11** A **Bo** Border	**21** I **Ku** Kumble	**30** SA **Pg** G. Pollock	**38** A **Pn** Ponting	**47** E **Am** Ames
7 I **Ga** Gavaskar / **12** A **Ws** S. Waugh / **15** NZ **Hd** Hadlee	**22** E **Be** Bedser	**31** P **Z** Zaheer	**39** A **Cl** Clarke	**48** E **Kn** Knott
8 NZ **Tu** Turner / **13** SA **Dr** Dravid / **16** SA **Ps** S. Pollock	**23** WI **Wl** Walsh	**32** A **Cg** G. Chappell	**40** SL **Sg** Sangakkara	**49** I **Bd** Bedi
9 SA **Sm** Smith / **14** WI **Ch** Chanderpaul / **17** SA **Ka** Kallis	**24** A **Mg** McGrath	**33** E **Gw** Gower	**41** I **Ko** Kohli	**50** E **An** Anderson

INNOVATORS & PIONEERS

95 E **G** Grace	**96** E **Rj** Ranjitsinhji	**97** SL **Ds** Dilshan	**98** WI **He** Headley	**99** SL **Rn** Ranatunga	**100** WI **Cn** Constantine
105 Af **Nb** Nabi	**106** E **Hf** Heyhoe Flint	**107** Z **Fl** Flower	**108** I **Dh** Dhoni	**109** E **Bq** Bosanquet	**110** A **Bu** Benaud

Number	Team	Symbol	Name
86	WI	Hl	Hall
87	A	Li	Lillee
51	E	Br	Brearley
52	WI	Gl	Gayle
53	E	Jd	Jardine
60	A	As	Armstrong
70	E	Js	Jessop
79	A	Or	O'Reilly
88	WI	Ro	Roberts
80	A	W	Warne
89	WI	Ho	Holding
54	P	Mn	Miandad
61	P	Af	Afridi
71	A	B	Bradman
81	A	Sp	Spofforth
90	WI	Mh	Marshall
55	P	Iz	Inzamam-ul-Haq
62	E	Bn	Barnes
66	WI	Gn	Greenidge
72	WI	Wk	Weekes
82	E	Lw	Larwood
91	WI	Ab	Ambrose
56	E	Ce	Close
63	E	Sn	Snow
67	SL	Jy	Jayasuriya
73	A	Ci	I. Chappell
76	WI	S	Sobers
83	A	Ln	Lindwall
92	P	Wa	Wasim
57	E	Gr	Greig
64	A	Th	Thomson
68	I	Sw	Sehwag
74	WI	Ld	Lloyd
77	E	Bt	Botham
84	E	Tm	Trueman
93	SA	Dn	Donald
58	E	Pt	Pietersen
59	SA	Cr	Cronje
65	P	Ak	Akhtar
69	A	Hn	Hayden
75	WI	Rv	V. Richards
78	A	Gi	Gilchrist
85	E	Ty	Tyson
94	SA	St	Steyn
101	WI	Wo	Worrell
102	E	Dl	D'Oliveira
103	A	Bv	Bevan
104	SA	Bl	Bland
111	P	Sq	Saqlain
112	SL	Mu	Muralitharan
113	SA	Nt	Ntini
114	SL	Ma	Malinga

ELEMENT KEY
TOP LEFT: ELEMENT NUMBER
TOP RIGHT: NATIONAL TEAM

Introduction

'New Zealand's balloon floats only when the gases are mixed just right.' So said the 1984 edition of *Wisden Cricketers' Almanack** in explaining how the Kiwi team, with its one or two superstars and a host of worker bees, could compete periodically with the best teams in the world. Cricket is a sport perpetually obsessed with the 'elements' that make up a team. It is a team game but not in the cohesive way of football or rugby. Instead, it is a series of individual battles – between batsman and bowler – that expose the character of the combatants and build the unique narrative of a contest.

Wisden Cricketers' Almanack has been published every year since 1864. It records and analyses any cricketing deed from around the world worth bothering with and has developed a worthy reputation for breadth, depth and editorial integrity. It is quoted plentifully throughout this book and is referred to simply as *Wisden*. Its digital offspring – not literally though they were once part of the same parent company – is ESPNcricinfo, which has also been an invaluable source of reference. It was the brainchild of one Indian and two British students based in the United States in the early 1990s who devised a way of sharing cricket scores with each other. Twenty-odd years on, ESPNcricinfo, based in Bangalore but with satellite offices around the globe, is the biggest single-sport website in the world and a go-to destination for live scores, live blogging, breaking news and trenchant analysis of everything going on in the cricket world.

Cricket is perfect material for a Periodic Table. It is an unwritten law of watching the game that when two or more are gathered together (whether that be at a match or simply in the pub), they shall discuss and argue about their favourite players: best, worst, silliest, oddest, hairiest and so on until the rain stops or the beer runs out. The fundamental problem with picking a cricket team is that you want twelve players but you can only have eleven. Six batsmen, a wicket-keeper, two spin bowlers and three fast bowlers. It doesn't add up. And that is why almost every cricket team in history is a compromise between what you want and what you can fit in. A batsman who bowls a bit of spin? Or the brilliant spinner who turns it a metre but who's afraid of the ball and would rather not have to bat at all? What will the pitch do – do we need an extra batsman or another bowling option? That is why the all-rounder – a player who is good enough at both batting and bowling (or wicket-keeping) to command a place for either discipline – is such a valuable commodity. Talking of spin bowling, it shouldn't be forgotten that cricket enjoys a minor and tangential relationship with the chemistry lab, Bunsen burner being used as rhyming slang for 'turner', or a pitch that will assist the spinner. 'Looks like a raging Bunsen today, Geoff.' Let's not even get into the science of swing bowling, and that's physics anyway.

Almost 4,000 men (and more than 1,000 women) have played international cricket since the first official Test match between Australia and England in 1877. Inevitably, then, the 114 elements of our table represent only a snapshot of the history of the international game. Cricket is a game of numbers as much as anything, so sorting the legends from the also-rans is a simple process. Except, of course, it isn't. Statistics tell only part of the story and sometimes they barely do that. Cricket fetishises stats more than any other international team sport: American football and baseball also like their numbers but for all their arcane fascination and complexities they are not played globally at an elite level, however much the nomenclature of the 'World Series' suggests otherwise.

Comparing players from different eras is fraught with difficulty and unfairness: the proliferation of international cricket in the last twenty years, for example, means that cumulative stats become skewed. Yet cricket's statistical framework allows you to have a pretty good go. Take Don Bradman, who is beyond argument the best batsman that ever lived. Because he played in an earlier era, plenty of others have scored more runs and played more matches than him. It's his killer batting average – 99.94, as every cricket nerd knows – that sets him apart and will do forever more.

The numbers, then, are great points of reference and provide the evidence for the arguments and the selections. But this would be a boring book if the sole criterion for inclusion was statistical. There has to be a degree of subjectivity, both in the framework of how the table is constructed and also in the selection of elements and players. There are many, many players who could have been selected for this book. Some who did get the final nod might seem slightly left-field choices but hopefully the argument for their inclusion is persuasive. Feel free to disagree – that is, after all, part of the fun.

Every player who appears in the table has played for their country. The primary field of reference is Test cricket, the oldest and still – just about – the most venerated form of the game. Matches can last up to five days and, yes, still end up being a draw. Both teams bat twice with essentially an unlimited time to complete their innings and in order to win a Test match you need to take all twenty of your opponent's wickets (unless they declared in their first innings but let's not get into that now). One of the most thrilling ways a Test can conclude is for the bowling team to be a wicket or two away from victory but finding the last couple of batsmen on the opposition (even though they have no hope of victory) providing stubborn and brave resistance. Draws might seem a bizarre concept to the uninitiated but they can be brilliant theatre.

One-day internationals (or ODIs) came into being in 1971 when a Test between Australia and England at Melbourne was washed out. The two teams convened for a one-day match which 46,000 people attended and a new international format was born. Each side bats once and has a limited number of (six-ball) overs. These days matches are standardised at fifty overs per side. The Cricket World Cup, which was first staged in 1975, is played over this format. Like its football and rugby union cousins, it occurs every four years.

Then there is Twenty20 (T20), born in England in 2003 through a desire to entice crowds back to domestic (county) cricket. It is essentially a pared down version of ODIs with only twenty overs per side, completed in three hours: with lots of six-hitting, dynamic fielding and varying degrees of razzmatazz, it is perfect for both television and a family evening out. The format was an instant success, even if, like the one-day game, many stick-in-the-muds viewed it 'not proper cricket'. Four years later, the first international tournament (World Twenty20) was staged in South Africa. India, who had previously been deeply skeptical of this brash new format, won it and were hooked: soon afterwards the Indian Premier League (IPL) was formed. As cricket met Bollywood, the international game changed forever: for decades the highest profile form of cricket had been nation versus nation contests but suddenly there was a conflict between that status quo and new T20 competitions involving city-based franchises. The IPL spawned similar leagues around the globe. Players, particularly those from smaller commercial markets like New Zealand and West Indies, were forced to choose between club and country. It is an ongoing conflict.

There is another conflict, too, between the established nations (there are ten countries who play Test cricket and England, Australia and India hold the financial and commercial power) and aspiring ones like

Ireland and Afghanistan. The latter are frustrated at what they perceive as a lack of respect and opportunity from the traditional cricket-playing countries. Because we are dealing with the entire scope of international cricket history and, by extension, majoring on achievements in Test cricket, the players selected in *The Periodic Table of Cricket* do come, almost exclusively, from the historically strong cricket nations. There is a degree of Anglo-centricity, not by design but more a function of England's roots as the home of cricket. It is also because there has been more first-class cricket (multi-day cricket that was really the only form of the game at elite level until the advent of limited-overs matches) played in England (and Wales) than anywhere else in the world. By the same token, there are many more post-war players in the table, reflecting the explosion of international cricket and the subsequent opportunities for modern players to raise the bar of achievement on a regular basis.

How the book works

The table is, in some respects, one massive all-time squad of players. Pick any XI out of that lot and you'd have a very decent side for whatever form of the game you were choosing to play.

Cricketers can in theory be categorised reasonably easily and neatly by their skill sets: Viv Richards was a top-order batsman, Dennis Lillee a fast bowler and so on. But it's never quite that straightforward because players, especially the really good ones, have more than one string to their bow. Not everyone can be easily pigeonholed. But as with the point earlier about numbers and statistics, this would be a dull book if players were arranged only by their primary skills.

In the real Periodic Table, elements are grouped by properties: elements close to each other share properties, while elements at opposite ends of the table are complementary opposites. So, how to create a similar framework for a table of cricketers? What is not being attempted is transposing cricketers on to the real Periodic Table: this not an exercise in deciding which player is an inert gas, for example. Instead, I have decided upon five categories for players based on on-field characteristics and, to an extent, off-field personality. Cricket reveals and exposes character like no other sport, in part because of the length of time the game takes to play, even in its briefest form. Often the on-field style is simply an extension of off-field personality but, in some cases, the two are at odds with each other.

While all the elements in our table are players, their profiles hopefully provide impressions of the game's rich and colourful history, whether that be the greatest matches, performances or controversies and conflicts, of which there have been plenty. From left to right, the main table moves from Defenders & Pragmatists through to Stylists & Entertainers, Mavericks & Rebels, and finishing with Aggressors & Enforcers. There is a separate block of Innovators & Pioneers. The table is mostly filled with all-time greats though some, particularly among the Innovators and Mavericks, are chosen for the impact on the game as a whole. There are few current players in the table and I have not considered anyone who made their international debut in 2010 or later. It just too speculative a judgement to make about highly talented young players such as England's Joe Root or Australia's Steve Smith at this early stage in their respective careers.

One could argue a case for some players to be in more than one category. Many great players, especially batsmen, have changed over time through necessity or design. When players first emerge on the scene, they may have a honeymoon period when their own self-confidence, energy and newness give them a flying start. Then opponents start working out to how to play against them and life becomes tougher. Batsmen might have to become more defensive and bowlers might have to reduce their pace to stay fit, or find more ingenious ways of getting batsmen out. The decision about the category in which players are placed is therefore a judgement call based on the overriding imprint of their careers.

Reading down each column of the table, the cricketers are placed, broadly speaking, by skill set: opening batsmen, middle-order batsmen, all-rounders (who mostly bat in the middle order), wicket-keepers, spin bowlers and fast bowlers. Within each of those sub-sets, players have been placed chronologically with older players at the top, the desired effect to present some sort of lineage or keeping of the flame through the ages.

Various interesting groupings and trends emerge. There are hotspots across the table, betraying the way the game's tactics and strategies have developed over time and also how different nationalities like to play their cricket. There are few wicket-keepers in the table. This is not an anti-gloveman prejudice but a judgement based on the truism that the best keepers go unnoticed, though eccentricity is often a trait and there are a few who would have been candidates for the Mavericks & Rebels. Over time it has been a wicket-keeper's batting ability that has set him apart, much to the chagrin of the purists.

So, there you have the methodology and the pre-emptive excuses. Now it is time for the literary umpire to call 'play'.

Defenders
&
Pragmatists

These are the men who stare you down, grind you down and think you out. We have a plethora of opening batsmen in this first part of table, whose qualities of patience, determination and bravery help fend off the thunderbolts from the opening bowlers among the Aggressors & Enforcers at the other end of the table, setting the platform for the Stylists & Entertainers to come.

The game has changed hugely over the past decade with the advent of Twenty20 and the old-school defensive opening batsman feels like a bit of a dinosaur. But there are a few of them still roaming planet cricket: Alastair Cook, for example, whose 836-minute 263 against Pakistan in late 2015 was the longest ever innings by an England batsman and the third longest in Test history. In the first column of the table, Cook is the fifth link in a proud, prolific and pragmatic chain of England opening batsmen stretching back to Jack Hobbs, who played his first Test in 1908.

But not all batsmen who come in after the openers can be or want to be dashers, launching sixes over the stands every five minutes. A good team needs a blend of different elements – a compound if you will. Plenty of batsmen have reined in their natural instincts or adjusted their techniques to rid their game of risk and ensure they are scoring the maximum runs for the team. Giving one's wicket away is still considered a great crime even in these times of all-out attack.

And then there are the bowlers. Not everyone can bowl 145 kph or spin it metres. 'Bowling dry' was one of the buzz-phrases of England's brief tenure at the top of the world Test match rankings in 2011–12, meaning they would simply try to stop the flow of the opposition's runs by exceptionally accurate bowling and astute field placements. Dead-eyed accuracy isn't a substitute for taking wickets: it's a means to an end.

Column 1

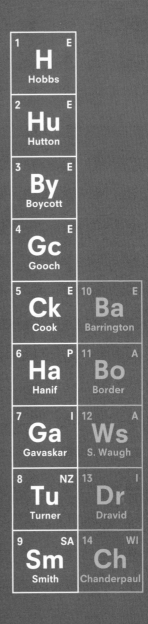

1	H	E
	Hobbs	

2	Hu	E
	Hutton	

3	By	E
	Boycott	

4	Gc	E
	Gooch	

5	Ck	E
	Cook	

10	Ba	E
	Barrington	

6	Ha	P
	Hanif	

11	Bo	A
	Border	

7	Ga	I
	Gavaskar	

12	Ws	A
	S. Waugh	

8	Tu	NZ
	Turner	

13	Dr	I
	Dravid	

9	Sm	SA
	Smith	

14	Ch	WI
	Chanderpaul	

JACK HOBBS

(England)

In an age when elite cricketers in England were divided distinctly between amateurs (stereotypically batsmen) and those who were paid to play the game (bowlers), John Berry Hobbs, always known as Jack Hobbs, broke the mould. Known as The Master, he was the first great professional, working-class batsman and his run-scoring feats still resonate today. In 1953, he was the first professional cricketer to be knighted and in 2000 he was the only Englishman to be named by *Wisden* as one of their five cricketers of the century. No one has scored more than his 61,760 first-class runs nor his 199 first-class hundreds – records that will never be broken given the diverse nature of the modern game. 'He seemed at his best to have two strokes and plenty of time for every ball bowled,' said his England teammate Frank Woolley.

During the first half of his career before the First World War, Hobbs was a stylish, attacking opening batsman. After 1918, by now in his late thirties, he reined himself in as these batting records, many of them held by W. G. Grace, appeared on the horizon. 'In those early days I had all the strokes. I hadn't the same fear of getting out,' Hobbs said. 'After the war ... it was the figures that counted all the time. Unless I'd got so many runs I'd failed. I was cautious.' He scored more than half of his centuries after the age of forty and remains the oldest man to score a Test century, aged forty-six against Australia at Melbourne in 1929.

In August 1925, the cricket world – not just England – became Hobbs-obsessed when the batsman scored back-to-back centuries at Taunton for Surrey against Somerset to pass Grace's career total of 126 hundreds. 'The climactic outpouring of enthusiasm for Hobbs showed how cricket in the 1920s, far more than today, was truly the national sport,' wrote Leo McKinstry in his 2011 biography of Hobbs.

LEN HUTTON

(England)

The embodiment of Yorkshire grit, Len Hutton was a prolific, technically correct, opening batsman for county and country, an Ashes-winning captain and a world record holder. 'A dour and painstaking character with a whimsical sense of humour,' was how the broadcaster and journalist Christopher Martin-Jenkins described him in *The Complete Who's Who of Test Cricketers*. Hutton was only twenty-two when he played his monumental innings of 364 against Australia at The Oval in 1938, batting for more than thirteen hours. It remained the highest individual Test score for almost twenty years until Garry Sobers surpassed it by a single run.

Hutton's embryonic international career might have been blighted by a serious injury in 1941. Having been recruited by the Army Physical Training Corps, he suffered a compound fracture of his left arm when he fell in the gym during commando training. His recovery took eight months in hospital after which time his left arm was two inches shorter than his right. His injury hampered his range of strokes but not his output nor resilience.

One of his most memorable innings came in a losing cause at Brisbane in the 1950–51 Ashes on a difficult pitch, known as a 'sticky dog' because of the effects of rain and heat on an uncovered surface. Chasing 193 for victory, Hutton's 62 not out in England's total of 122 is remembered as one of the most skilful by any England batsman. Hutton 'played the turning or lifting ball with the ease of a master craftsman', wrote *Wisden*.

In the early 1950s Hutton became England's first full-time professional captain, the role having previously been the preserve of the university-educated amateur players. His leadership style was considered 'sound rather than venturesome', according to Norman Yardley, a Yorkshire teammate and a predecessor as England captain. But Hutton captained England to two era-defining Ashes series wins. The first in 1953, the Queen's coronation year, tapped into a mood of national celebration, not least because England hadn't beaten Australia in a series for twenty years. Eighteen months later in Australia, they retained the urn despite losing the first Test heavily.

GEOFFREY BOYCOTT

(England)

At the crease, Geoff Boycott was one of the most technically correct, risk-averse compilers of runs the game has known. Off the field, both as player and later as a pundit, he was a divisive figure who roused extraordinary passions for and against. To his supporters, his single-minded approach to batsmanship was a sign of his greatness. To others, especially in Yorkshire where the bizarre Boycott soap opera played out in the 1970s, he was a selfish troublemaker. In that respect, he could be seen as a maverick but ultimately his craft and determination as an opening batsman is the predominant quality to be considered. Meticulous in both his appearance and his technique, he was as stylish as any fundamentally defensive batsman could be.

Boycott's highest Test score was 246 not out in 1967 against India on his home ground at Leeds. After batting for almost ten hours he was dropped for the next match for slow scoring. He scored twenty-two Test centuries in 108 matches – the joint most for England until Alastair Cook surpassed it in 2012 – and could have played more, missing thirty Tests in the mid 1970s through self-imposed exile. He returned triumphantly in 1977 to help England regain the Ashes and reached the pinnacle of his hundredth first-class hundred at Leeds against Australia. It was a highly emotional moment for him and his Yorkshire public. He would score another fifty centuries before his retirement in 1982, putting him level with another great Yorkshire opener, Herbert Sutcliffe. Only four batsmen have scored more first-class hundreds in history; they were all essentially pre-war players.

GRAHAM GOOCH

(England)

'I don't coach batting, I coach run-making,' said Graham Gooch in an interview for *All Out Cricket* magazine in late 2013, during his time as England's specialist batting coach. And he should know. When he retired in 1997, it was calculated that he had scored more runs – including all scores, one-day and first-class, at domestic as well as international level – than anyone in the history of the game. He was England's all-time leading Test run-scorer for more than twenty years until his protégé Alastair Cook usurped him in 2015.

Having received no formal coaching until his late teens, Gooch started out as a dashing middle-order player for Essex but finished up, after twenty-four years at the top level, as a punishingly prolific opening batsman. He became the ultimate pragmatist, working hard on his game and his personal fitness to eke every last drop out of his considerable talent.

Gooch's England Test career began with a pair of ducks against Australia in 1975 and was interrupted by a three-year ban in the early 1980s for joining a rebel tour of apartheid South Africa but by the early 1990s he was officially rated as the best batsman in the world. The defining innings of the period was his 154 not out at Leeds in 1991 against a still-dominant West Indies in a match containing only three other scores of more than 50. In 2015 it was selected by a panel judges in *All Out Cricket* magazine as the best post-war innings by an England batsman.

Gooch got better with age – and experience. He scored more than half of his Test runs after his thirty-fifth birthday, including his famous 333 against India at Lord's in 1990, the third highest in history by an England batsman. He was equally adept in the one-day game, as he showed with a match-winning century against India in the semi-final of the 1987 World Cup.

ALASTAIR COOK

(England)

In 2015 Alastair Cook became England's leading Test run-scorer and later joined a select group of England captains (the others being W. G. Grace and Mike Brearley) to have won two home Ashes series. It is not his captaincy that defines this stubborn left-handed opener, though, but his powers of concentration, his unflappable temperament and his capacity for compiling long innings in an era where the crash and bang of Twenty20 cricket has also become the norm in five-day Test matches too.

Cook himself attributes part of this ability to the discipline and rigour instilled at an early age when he was a chorister at St Paul's Cathedral. Equally the hours spent in the nets at Essex's Chelmsford headquarters with his long-time mentor Graham Gooch should not be underestimated. It was fitting that Cook should overtake Gooch's record even though Cook said he 'wouldn't put myself anywhere near his class'.

It seemed inevitable that Cook would be the man to become England's leading run-scorer right from the moment in 2006 when he made a century on his Test debut against India at Nagpur. The twenty-one-year-old had flown all the way from England's second-string tour in the Caribbean as an emergency replacement for the injured England captain Michael Vaughan and 'unveiled a compact technique and tremendous temperament', according to *Wisden*. The match was also the start of a formidable opening partnership with Andrew Strauss, who in 2010–11 led England to their first Ashes series victory in Australia for twenty-four years. Cook was a cornerstone of England's 3-1 triumph, racking up an astonishing 766 runs in seven innings as Australia were ground into submission. It was the highest total by an England batsman in an Ashes series since Wally Hammond's 905 in 1928–29.

HANIF MOHAMMAD

(Pakistan)

It is believed that Hanif Mohammad, Pakistan's first great cricketer, was a pioneer of the reverse sweep shot, though whether that honour actually belongs to his brother Mushtaq is lost in the mists of time. Innovation, however, is not his legacy: rather it is two huge scores that remain monuments to run-making. Hanif put Pakistan cricket on the map and his family's connection with the game is the most remarkable of any country. Three of his brothers played Test cricket as did his son Shoaib. A host of other family members have also played first-class cricket.

In January 1958 in Barbados, Pakistan followed on against West Indies, 473 runs behind. That the Test was drawn was due entirely to Hanif playing the longest innings in Test history. He was only twenty-eight runs short of the then highest score but his batting marathon of sixteen hours, ten minutes remains a record. 'It was an innings of the greatest skill, but played with utmost discipline and dedication. He applied the most masterful technique, but guarded that with fierce concentration, traits which he exhibited through his career,' wrote one of Hanif's opponents that day, Garry Sobers, in the foreword to Hanif's autobiography.

Eleven months later, Hanif passed Don Bradman's record for the highest first-class score, 454 not out, which had been set back in 1930. Playing for Karachi against Bahawalpur in the semi-final of Pakistan's domestic competition, Hanif came to the crease late on the first day of four after Bahawalpur had been bowled out cheaply. By the close of day two he had 255, his own highest score. On and on he batted, urged to pursue Bradman's record by his brother, Wazir, the Karachi captain. After tea on

the third day, Hanif passed Bradman's record in front of
a crowd of about a thousand. Then with two balls of the
day left, he was on 496. He wanted to get to 500, partly
because it was uncharted territory and partly because
he feared his brother would declare the innings. Having
moved on to 498, Hanif was run out going for the second
run to reach the milestone. His record stood until 1994
when Brian Lara broke it playing for Warwickshire in
England's County Championship.

SUNIL GAVASKAR

(India)

Many batsmen were cowed by the four-pronged West
Indies pace attack that ruled the cricketing world through
relentless accuracy and the threat of physical harm in
the 1970s and 1980s. But not Sunil Gavaskar: one of the
greatest of all opening batsmen and certainly India's
best batsman until the emergence of Sachin Tendulkar.
As Harsha Bhogle, the voice of Indian cricket, wrote: 'Till
he came along, with a boyish mop of hair and a defiant
attitude beneath, Indians had been told that they could
not play fast bowling.'

Short of stature, with a near-perfect, compact batting
technique, Gavaskar was certainly not a dour player but
established a well-founded reputation for powers of
resilience and concentration. He was twenty-one when
he was called up for his debut series in 1970–71 in the
Caribbean and scored 774 runs in four Tests at a colossal
average of 154.80. It remains (at the time of writing) the
most runs scored in a series by an Indian batsman. While
the West Indies bowling attack was not at that stage fully
formed into the world-beating force it later became,
Gavaskar continued to flourish against that particular
opponent, scoring thirteen centuries and averaging
sixty-five over the course of his career. Remember, too,
that he was playing before the invention of the protective
helmet, even if he was something of a pioneer by wearing

a curious, specially designed skull protector that fitted beneath his trademark sun hat.

Gavaskar was the first Test batsman to score 10,000 runs and in December 1983 overtook Don Bradman's haul of twenty-nine Test centuries, a record that had stood since the Australian's retirement in 1948. That he broke the record with 236 not out against West Indies – the record score for an Indian batsman at the time – just emphasises his appetite for run-scoring.

Gavaskar took his reputation for defensive solidity to absurd lengths in the opening match of the inaugural World Cup in 1975. With India set 335 to win off 60 overs by host nation England, Gavaskar showed no inclination to chase the total. Instead, he batted through the entire innings, facing 174 balls for 36 not out as India lost by 202 runs. It was a bizarre display that incurred the displeasure of India's team management and supporters alike. Eight years later, however, he was part of the India side that shocked holders West Indies at Lord's to win the World Cup for the first time.

GLENN TURNER

(New Zealand)

In the amateur world of 1960s and 1970s New Zealand cricket, Glenn Turner took a different view. He was a professional in every sense of the word. He carved a hugely successful career for Worcestershire through the 1970s and early 1980s and even passed up New Zealand's 1978 tour of England to stay with his county side. It was not a decision to endear him to New Zealand's cricket authorities and he would later fall out with them again after a period as captain. Just as compatriot Richard Hadlee dedicated himself to the pursuit of unseating batsmen, so Turner had a similarly single-minded pursuit of crease occupation and run accumulation. Pale and slight, he did not cut an imposing figure at the crease but bowlers were soon cursing his straight bat and his immaculate defensive technique.

His Test career began modestly but three years in, at Kingston in 1972, he scored almost sixty per cent of his side's first-innings runs against West Indies: 223 not out (batting the whole innings) out of 386. That innings was one of four double centuries he made on New Zealand's tour of the Caribbean, including 259 at Georgetown in the fourth Test. He scored centuries for Worcestershire against all the other sixteen first-class counties and also against New Zealand. In 1982 he became only the second non-Englishman to reach a hundred first-class centuries. He achieved the milestone in appropriately substantial fashion, making a century before lunch for Worcestershire against their rivals Warwickshire and then progressing to 311 not out, the highest score of his career.

GRAEME SMITH

(South Africa)

Appointed captain of South Africa at the age of twenty-two in the wake of the Hansie Cronje match-fixing scandal, Graeme Smith forged an exceptional career out of a granite will. A left-handed batsman of seemingly limited ability and heavy leg-side bias, Smith is the only South African to have scored five Test double-centuries. Another indication of his mental toughness is the number of match-winning centuries (four, a record) he scored in Test-match run-chases.

When he started his international career, Smith was abused by Australians and when he became captain he was mocked by his English opposite number, Nasser Hussain, referring to Smith as Greg rather than Graeme before the sides met in 2003 for only the third match of Smith's captaincy. After Smith scored 277 and 259 in the space of three innings, however, everyone knew his name. In 2008, he led South Africa to their first Test series win in England since 1965 and only a few months later skippered his side to their first ever series victory in Australia. He captained South Africa in 109 of his 117 Tests.

Column 2

1 E **H** Hobbs	
2 E **Hu** Hutton	
3 E **By** Boycott	
4 E **Gc** Gooch	

5 E **Ck** Cook	**10** E **Ba** Barrington	
6 P **Ha** Hanif	**11** A **Bo** Border	
7 I **Ga** Gavaskar	**12** A **Ws** S. Waugh	**15** NZ **Hd** Hadlee
8 NZ **Tu** Turner	**13** I **Dr** Dravid	**16** SA **Ps** S. Pollock
9 SA **Sm** Smith	**14** WI **Ch** Chanderpaul	**17** SA **Ka** Kallis

KEN BARRINGTON

(England)

Ken Barrington was a heroic figure for Surrey and England through the 1950s and 1960s. A cheery soul with a reputation for mixed metaphors and malapropisms, he was a middle-order batsman who remodelled his batting style at the start of the 1960s from stylish convention to an open-chested stance that he described in his autobiography, *Running into Hundreds,* as 'plain ugly'. That switch, fundamentally from attack to defence, confirmed his reputation as a blocker – even though he had the habit of trying to reach a century by hitting a six. He was once dropped for slow scoring when he took more than seven hours to score 137. But he had an impressive conversion rate of half-centuries into centuries – one of the hallmarks of a top player – and his Test average of fifty-eight is the sixth highest of all time.

The son of a soldier, Barrington was a fiercely patriotic man. The Australian wicket-keeper Wally Grout once said, 'Whenever Ken walked to the wicket, I thought a Union Jack was trailing behind him.' Barrington later became a trusted and popular assistant manager for England. His sudden death from a heart attack in Barbados during a Test between England and West Indies in 1981 was a severe blow to England's players and mourned throughout the cricket world.

ALLAN BORDER

(Australia)

A reluctant captain, Allan Border dragged Australia up by their bootstraps in the 1980s after retirements and rebel tours to South Africa had left this great cricket nation on its knees. Tough, brave and uncompromising, Border took the view after a particularly shaming Ashes series loss in England in 1985 that his team needed to get serious, and then get even. Four years later Australia returned, unsmiling and unbeatable, turning England over 4-0. Australia would not lose another Ashes series until 2005.

Short and feisty, Border was the ultimate Aussie battler. 'Throughout his career, Border often managed to be both a great cricketer and an ordinary bloke,' wrote Mark Ray, the former Tasmania cricketer, in *Border and Beyond*. 'It was his greatest attraction to the fans in the stands.'

Border's durability was legendary. A left-handed batsman with a limited range of shots, he won few points for artistic merit but top marks for technical difficulty. Despite playing in an era of great fast bowlers and the attendant physical dangers that brought for batsmen, he holds the record for most consecutive Test matches (153) and the most consecutive Tests as captain (93). In 1994 at Adelaide against South Africa, close to the end of his career, he became the first batsman to pass 11,000 Test runs during an innings that, in many ways, summed him up: eighty-four, made in five hours and thirty-eight minutes, containing only three boundaries. And Australia won, of course.

STEVE WAUGH

(Australia)

'The man's a machine,' wrote Gideon Haigh dryly in his review of Steve Waugh's 801-page autobiography *Out of My Comfort Zone*. And it wasn't even Waugh's first book, not by a long chalk. That, as Haigh observed, was Waugh to a tee: churn it out, leave it all out on the page – or previously, the pitch. Few cricketers in history have fulfilled their talent quite to the exceptional extent of Waugh.

He entered the stage in the late 1980s at a transitional stage for Australia. He started out as an all-rounder who bowled jaunty medium pace and, when batting, liked to take on the bowlers. He left the stage, almost twenty years later, an entirely different cricketer: Australia's most successful captain and holder of a variety of batting records. Initially mocked as 'not even the best all-rounder in his own family', Waugh lost his place in the Australian side to his younger twin Mark, a batsman of rare style and flourish. Steve set about rebuilding his game, working out ways to succeed. This involved eschewing the hook shot against pace bowlers and trying to eliminate all risk from his game. He batted deep in his crease, relied on two or three shots, most potently a sort of square drive that was lashed through point whenever he was given any width. In Jamaica in 1995 he and his brother put on 231 together (Steve made 200, Mark 126) to seal Australia's epochal victory over West Indies, who had not lost a Test series for fifteen years.

Steve Waugh was already one-day captain by the time he took the Test job in 1999. He led Australia in fifteen of their record sixteen consecutive Test victories that year and won the World Cup to boot. His leadership was defined by all-out aggression, both in terms of encouraging his batsmen to score as quickly as possible and also as an intimidating, sometimes confrontational presence on the field.

RAHUL DRAVID

(India)

Rahul Dravid played his entire career in the shadow of one of the greatest batsmen of all time, Sachin Tendulkar, yet he was in no way diminished as a result. If anything, the contrast between the two cast Dravid in an even greater light. He spent much of his sixteen-year career batting at number three with the star turn, Tendulkar, at four. As such, his dismissal would often be greeted by elation among the thousands of Indians who had come to pay homage to their hero.

But this curious phenomenon never fazed Dravid, nor did much else. His nickname of The Wall only told part of the story. At his best, he was nigh on impossible to dislodge but he was also pleasing on the eye – a tall right-hander in the classical style. He made ninety-five on his Test debut at Lord's in 1996 and would play 164 Tests in all (including one for a World XI in 2005), a total bettered by only four other players in history. He also played 344 one-day internationals, including the 2003 World Cup campaign when India reached the final.

Later that year, Dravid batted for 835 minutes across two innings of a gripping match at Adelaide, scoring 233 and 72 not out, as India won a Test in Australia for the first time in twenty-two years. In the 2011 series in England, which India lost 4-0, Dravid opened the batting against an England side that would become the No.1-ranked side in the world by the end of the summer. He made 461 in four Tests including three centuries, facing almost 1,000 deliveries in the process.

Dravid was a man for all seasons, and all conditions. His Test batting average was slightly higher away from home than it was in India. He scored centuries against all nine Test opponents and double-centuries against five of them. His studious approach to batting was replicated in his off-field demeanour. He became an increasingly erudite ambassador for the game as cricket, particularly in India, became ever more commercialised.

SHIVNARINE CHANDERPAUL

(West Indies)

In the post-Brian Lara collapse of West Indies cricket, Shivnarine Chanderpaul was the rock, albeit of a very peculiar geological formation. Defying all the standard conventions that cricket is a side-on game, this diminutive Guyanese left-hander turned his stance ninety degrees so it appeared as if he was facing a bowler coming in from square leg. You could make a case for Chanderpaul being a maverick – he did after all once mistakenly shoot a policeman in the hand, thinking he was an intruder. But the manifestation of his quirks was defiance – twenty-one years of it – and more than

11,000 Test runs, many scored with frustrating flicks and deflections.

It took Chanderpaul twenty-two Tests to score his first Test century and six more to make a second but by the time the West Indies board called time on his career in 2015 – in a predictably messy and unsatisfactory way – he had made thirty hundreds, along with sixty-six half-centuries. He was at his best against the best, never more so than in 2012 against Australia when, aged thirty-seven, he became the second West Indian, after Brian Lara, to pass 10,000 Test runs. He made a century, three fifties and then two more half-centuries on a subsequent tour to England before moving on to Bangladesh for a career-best 203 not out. His Test average in the calendar year was ninety-eight.

Column 3

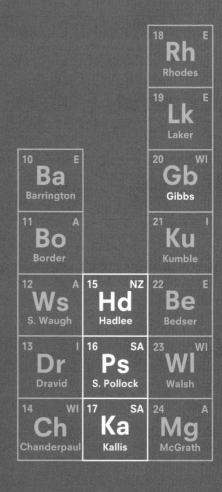

		18 E **Rh** Rhodes
		19 E **Lk** Laker
10 E **Ba** Barrington		20 WI **Gb** Gibbs
11 A **Bo** Border		21 I **Ku** Kumble
12 A **Ws** S. Waugh	15 NZ **Hd** Hadlee	22 E **Be** Bedser
13 I **Dr** Dravid	16 SA **Ps** S. Pollock	23 WI **Wl** Walsh
14 WI **Ch** Chanderpaul	17 SA **Ka** Kallis	24 A **Mg** McGrath

RICHARD HADLEE

(New Zealand)

Richard Hadlee began, by his own admission, as something of an erratic fast bowler, but went on to shape himself into a deadly, precise seamer who unpicked batsmen's defences with forensic analysis. He elevated New Zealand from also-rans to contenders almost single-handedly during the 1980s and in early 1990 became the first man to take 400 Test wickets. A devastating force in English county cricket, too, with Nottinghamshire, he stood shoulder to shoulder with the other great all-rounders of the age: Ian Botham, Imran Khan and Kapil Dev.

Known as Paddles for his large, splayed feet, Hadlee's early bowling was marked by a long run-up with a quirky side-step at the start. He soon reduced his approach to the crease and his pace, to an extent, while developing unerring control. Modelling himself on Dennis Lillee, Hadlee's classical, side-on delivery stride and follow-through were certainly reminiscent of the great Australian, even if he did not replicate Lillee's snarling menace. Hadlee's approach was serious and surgical. 'While New Zealanders admired his ability they stopped short of hero worship,' wrote the veteran New Zealand journalist Don Cameron. 'Hadlee was forming his career in his own fashion: determined, seeking perfection, but not with the homespun warmth that New Zealanders seek in their sporting heroes.'

In 1974, he took seven wickets at Christchurch as New Zealand beat Australia in a Test for the first time. At Wellington three years later he took ten in the match to help defeat England, again a New Zealand first. There was plenty more new ground to be broken: New Zealand's first Test win in England in 1983; their first series win there in 1986; and back-to-back wins over Australia in 1985-86, including a nine-wicket haul at Brisbane. In 1990 he became the first cricketer to be knighted while still playing.

SHAUN POLLOCK

(South Africa)

With Allan Donald breathing fire at one end and Shaun Pollock asking polite but searching questions from the other, South Africa had a potent and complementary new-ball attack for seven years through the late 1990s and early 2000s. Pollock's father, Peter, also bowled for South Africa while his uncle, Graeme, was their country's greatest batsman so the gene pool was certainly promising.

Pollock Junior had a classical high action and by delivering from so close to the stumps bowled a very tight off-stump line that provided batsmen with a constant examination. He made his debut against England in 1995 when his father Peter was chairman of selectors, but there was no hint of nepotism. 'The latest sprig of South Africa's most famous cricketing family belied his innocent looks and manner with the sharpness of his bowling, mostly fast in-swing, including some very well-aimed bouncers,' reported *Wisden*. A few months later he went to England to play county cricket for Warwickshire and took four wickets in four balls in his first match. He often reserved his best for facing England (91 of his 421 Test wickets came against them) and was unplayable on conditions, home or away, that assisted lateral movement.

Pollock's stint as captain of South Africa in the early 2000s was, sadly for him, defined by his side's embarrassing exit from the group stage of their home World Cup in 2003 when his own batsmen were unclear about the amount of runs they needed to beat Sri Lanka after rain had forced the target to be revised.

JACQUES KALLIS

(South Africa)

With the physique of a rugby No.8 and the equable temperament of a surgeon, Jacques Kallis was a towering constant in South African cricket for almost twenty years until his retirement in 2014: a 'broad-shouldered colossus', according to the South African writer Telford Vice.

The combined physical requirements to bat in the top order and bowl at a decent pace are considerable enough without contemplating the extent of Kallis's success or the longevity of his career. Whereas some fine players burn brightly and then burn out, Kallis's flame was always flickering until he decided to snuff it out. No South African has scored more than his 13,289 Test runs (also the third highest in the all-time global list) nor his 11,579 one-day runs. He is the only cricketer to have scored more than 10,000 in both Test and ODI formats while also taking more than 200 wickets in both formats. He is also fifth on South Africa's list of all-time Test wicket-takers and third in their one-day list. And yet there's more – only two men in history have taken more than his 200 Test catches, most of them snaffled without fuss or flourish in the slips.

Kallis's game, both with bat and ball, was based on strength and power, rather than finesse. But it was a very measured power that ground opponents down rather than blowing them away. That style – chilling rather than thrilling – provoked accusations that he was a selfish, rather than team-orientated, player. Certainly he did cash in against weaker sides and his record against stronger nations such as Australia and England, even when South Africa were winning, was moderate.

Column 4

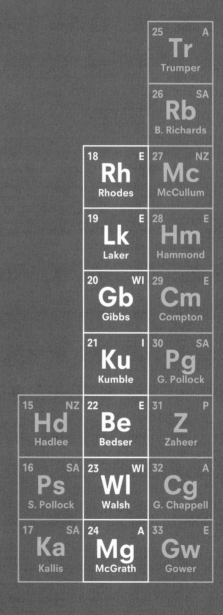

25 A **Tr** Trumper	
26 SA **Rb** B. Richards	
18 E **Rh** Rhodes	27 NZ **Mc** McCullum
19 E **Lk** Laker	28 E **Hm** Hammond
20 WI **Gb** Gibbs	29 E **Cm** Compton
21 I **Ku** Kumble	30 SA **Pg** G. Pollock
15 NZ **Hd** Hadlee	22 E **Be** Bedser	31 P **Z** Zaheer
16 SA **Ps** S. Pollock	23 WI **Wl** Walsh	32 A **Cg** G. Chappell
17 SA **Ka** Kallis	24 A **Mg** McGrath	33 E **Gw** Gower

WILFRED RHODES

(England)

Described by the great *Guardian* writer Neville Cardus as 'Yorkshire cricket personified', Rhodes was a left-arm spinner and opening batsman whose career implausibly spanned thirty-two years from 1898 to 1930. That longevity yielded some eye-watering records that are unlikely ever to be broken. No bowler has taken more than his 4,204 first-class wickets nor played in more than his 1,110 matches. He also scored almost 40,000 runs. He passed 1,000 runs in a season twenty-one times and 100 wickets in a season twenty-three times. Yorkshire won the County Championship four times in the first five years of Rhodes's career.

Cardus also described Rhodes as 'shrewd' and 'dour' while Don Bradman wrote: 'I can still picture the economy of his action. The great accuracy and cunning of his bowling.' Rhodes played the first of his fifty-eight Tests in 1899 and the last in 1930. In 1926 he was recalled by England, only a couple of months shy of his forty-ninth birthday, five years after his previous Test. It was the fifth and final match of the Ashes, with the series poised at 0-0. Rhodes took four for forty-four in the second innings, helping to secure a famous win, and the urn, for Percy Chapman's England side.

JIM LAKER

(England)

A detached, understated Yorkshireman, Jim Laker was a classical off-spinner with great control and relentless accuracy. He made his name at Surrey where he formed a devastating partnership with his 'spin twin' Tony Lock, helping the county to seven successive County Championship titles in the 1950s. The pair also played together twenty-four times for England, never more famously than at Manchester in 1956 when Laker accounted for nineteen of the twenty Australia wickets in the match. Lock took the other one.

Laker's scarcely believable bowling figures of nineteen wickets for ninety runs in that match (nine for thirty-seven in the first innings, then ten for fifty-three in the second) are among the most iconic statistics in cricket history. No bowler had ever taken every wicket in a Test innings before and it would be forty-three years until anyone did it again (Anil Kumble bowling out Pakistan in 1999). The 1956 match itself was a dramatic one with rain pushing the conclusion right to the wire on the final day, all the while with controversy simmering about the state of the pitch. Laker and Lock bowled in tandem with Lock unluckily spinning the ball past the Australian bats on many occasions until Laker trapped the Australian wicket-keeper Len Maddocks lbw to complete his unprecedented haul. 'He earned his triumph by remarkable control of length and spin,' said *Wisden*, 'and it is doubtful whether he bowled more than six bad length balls throughout the match.'

Laker's response to his seminal achievement was to take his sweater from the umpire, throw it over his shoulder and walk from the field with barely a flicker of emotion. Later that evening, he stopped in a pub on the way home from Manchester. As he sat drinking a beer and eating a sandwich, listening to the crowded bar talking about the Test match, no one so much as recognised him. He was a willing non-celebrity. He later became a lugubrious but astute television commentator.

LANCE GIBBS

(West Indies)

For five years Lance Gibbs was the leading Test wicket-taker, having become, in 1975, only the second bowler in history – and the first spinner – to reach 300 wickets. Tall and lithe, he was an off-spinner with a relatively unusual chest-on action. He spun it hard and his height enabled him to extract good bounce. He took five wickets in an innings eighteen times and, most astonishingly of all, conceded runs at a rate of under two per over.

He was at his most productive in the early 1960s. He took eight wickets, including three in four balls, in his first Test in Australia, at Sydney, the third of the gripping 1960–61 series. Against India at Bridgetown in 1962, he sealed a series victory for West Indies with an amazing spell of bowling – eight wickets for only six runs in 15.3 overs, fourteen of which were maidens. No West Indies spinner before or since even got close to 200 wickets and only Carl Hooper, a batsman who bowled part-time off-spin, has taken 100 or more wickets since Gibbs's time.

ANIL KUMBLE

(India)

'I didn't see him turn a single ball from leg to off. I don't believe we will have much problem with him,' claimed the England manager Keith Fletcher about Anil Kumble after a scouting mission before his side's tour to India in 1993. Kumble went on to take twenty-one wickets in the three Test matches, all of which India won. Fletcher would not be the last to underestimate this tall, bespectacled wrist-spin bowler. Kumble's effectiveness lay in accuracy and bounce – or 'kick' – off the pitch, using top spin rather than the traditional leg-spinner's approach of spinning the ball away from the right-handed batsman.

At Delhi in 1999, Kumble bowled India to victory over rivals Pakistan, itself an achievement worthy of hero status. But he did it by becoming only the second man in Test history to take all ten wickets in an innings. 'All I had to do was pitch in the right area, mix up my pace and spin, and trap the batsmen,' said Kumble afterwards. Pakistan had been 101 for no wicket until Kumble changed ends and took six for fifteen in forty-four balls. With one wicket remaining, pace bowler Javagal Srinath was instructed by India's captain Mohammad Azharuddin to bowl a wayward line, in order that Kumble could complete his remarkable feat. This he duly did when Wasim Akram was caught at short leg by V. V. S. Laxman.

Kumble proved to be a capable – and brave – tail-end batsman. In Antigua in 2002, he suffered a broken jaw from a ball by Merv Dillon, the West Indies fast bowler. With his head wrapped in bandages, Kumble returned to the field to bowl fourteen successive overs. At The Oval in 2007, he scored his one Test hundred, batting at No.8, to help put India on the way to only their third series victory in England.

ALEC BEDSER

(England)

Alec Bedser was 'the epitome of the English seam bowler', according to his *Wisden* obituary. Powerfully built, he was an identical twin and his brother Eric, from whom he was inseparable, also played successfully as an all-rounder for Surrey during the county's period of dominance in the 1950s.

Alec first played Test cricket in England's first match after the Second World War, against India. He started as he meant to go on, taking eleven wickets in both of his first two Tests. Those immediate post-war years were tough for England, as wartime had either prematurely ended careers or taken a physical toll on others. Bedser himself was twenty-eight when he made his debut. Until the emergence of Fred Trueman in the early 1950s, Bedser carried England's pace attack, a burden he bore with skill and fortitude. At Adelaide in January 1947, he dismissed Don Bradman for nought with a leg-cutter – a ball moving off the pitch from leg to off, which was Bedser's surprise delivery to counter his standard ball, the nagging in-swinger. Bradman described the ball as 'I think, the finest ever to take my wicket'. Bedser got the great man on five other occasions during his career. In the first Test of the

1953 Ashes, he became England's leading Test wicket-taker, a record he would hold for almost ten years.

After his retirement in 1960, he became an England tour manager and later a team selector for twenty-three years. Downbeat, grudging with praise, he could come across as a curmudgeon. 'If he says you're not bad, you're one of the three best in the world,' said fellow selector Doug Insole.

COURTNEY WALSH

(West Indies)

Wearing an expression of apparently perpetual surprise, Courtney Walsh was the antithesis of the 'nasty fasties' produced with such regularity by the West Indies. Tall, tireless and immensely popular, he served one of the longest apprentices in international cricket. For the best part of ten years he was the first or second-change pace bowler and it was not until 1993, after Malcolm Marshall had retired, that he graduated to share the new ball with Curtly Ambrose. The pair formed a fearsome and complementary partnership until Ambrose's retirement in 2000 when these two great bowlers left the field at The Oval with arms draped over round each other's shoulders.

Nasser Hussain, the former England captain, has asserted that he found Walsh a more difficult bowler to face than Ambrose, who would generally be regarded as the greater of the two. Hussain's claim was based on Walsh's natural tendency to deliver the ball from a wide angle – not to mention a terrific height – and then straighten the ball off the pitch, making it hard for the batsman to pick up the line of the ball.

Walsh simply got better with age and experience. He took 341 of his 519 Test wickets after his thirtieth birthday and at a marginally improved average on the first eight years of his Test career. In March 2000 against Zimbabwe on his home ground of Sabina Park in Kingston, he passed Kapil Dev's mark of 434 to be become the leading Test wicket-taker of all time – a testament to his skill, fitness and determination.

GLENN McGRATH

(Australia)

There was no mystery to facing Glenn McGrath, just misery. Tall and slim, he was not especially fast. Nor did he have an armoury full of wicked variations. But he had an uncanny ability to deliver the ball, time after time, on a spot just outside off stump where the batsman didn't know whether to play forward or back, whether to attack the ball or let it pass to the wicket-keeper. The yin-and-yang partnership he formed with Shane Warne in the 1990s and 2000s was a central plank in Australia's domination of the Test and one-day arenas during that period.

McGrath came late to cricket, which was a contributing factor to his longevity and lack of serious injuries. Born in the New South Wales town of Dubbo, he didn't start playing the game properly until he was fifteen and even then his club captain 'thought I couldn't bowl'. At seventeen, he was spotted by the former Australian player Doug Walters, who persuaded McGrath to move to Sydney to further his cricket. This he did while living in a caravan. In 1993 he took five wickets on his New South Wales debut and was playing for Australia later in the year.

McGrath made life uncomfortable for the very best batsmen, though none quite so much as the England opening batsman, Mike Atherton, whom McGrath dismissed nineteen times in seventeen Test matches. 'It was a one-way contest,' said Atherton. Even the West Indian Brian Lara, one of the two or three greatest batsmen of the era, fell to McGrath on seventeen occasions. At Lord's in 1997, on his first tour of England, he took eight wickets for thirty-eight runs as England were rolled over for only seventy-seven. McGrath was expert in the unique conditions at Lord's with its notorious slope.

In 2005, playing in a one-off Test against a World XI, he passed Courtney Walsh's record for the most career wickets by a pace bowler. He finished his career with 563 wickets, signing off in 2007 on his home patch, Sydney Cricket Ground, after a 5-0 Ashes whitewash alongside fellow retirees Warne and Justin Langer.

Stylists &
Entertainers

'I played a certain way, and I still enjoy watching the players who make it look easy,' says the former England batsman, David Gower. He's not the only one. Cricket, more than most professional team sports, respects the opponent.

If you are a paying spectator you can still go home happy if you've seen an unforgettable innings or a mesmeric spell of bowling even if it's not from a player on your team. But style over substance? 'It's not how, it's how many,' says Ricky Ponting, Australia's leading Test run-scorer. It's a batting truism but Ponting is being disingenuous or falsely modest. He was both brilliant to watch and, once he'd matured from being a youthful firebrand, a rock for his team. Batsmen are prone to fetishise style and technique. There is undoubtedly something aesthetically delightful about a perfectly played cover drive, for example: head over the ball, body balanced, weight shifting forward, straight bat flowing through in an arc and, most importantly, the ball whistling along the turf to the boundary.

Bowlers, as they will always tell you, get a raw deal in the entertainment stakes – and in life generally. 'It's a batsman's game,' they'll tell you, and broadly speaking they're right. Many bowlers would balk at the idea that style matters. It's more about the craft. Artisans rather than artists. There aren't many bowlers in this chapter but they're master craftsmen.

Column 5

	25 A **Tr** Trumper	
	26 SA **Rb** B. Richards	34 NZ **Cw** Crowe
18 E **Rh** Rhodes	27 NZ **Mc** McCullum	35 I **T** Tendulkar
19 E **Lk** Laker	28 E **Hm** Hammond	36 WI **Lr** Lara
20 WI **Gb** Gibbs	29 E **Cm** Compton	37 A **Wm** M. Waugh
21 I **Ku** Kumble	30 SA **Pg** G. Pollock	38 A **Pn** Ponting
22 E **Be** Bedser	31 P **Z** Zaheer	39 A **Cl** Clarke
23 WI **Wl** Walsh	32 A **Cg** G. Chappell	40 SL **Sg** Sangakkara
24 A **Mg** McGrath	33 E **Gw** Gower	41 I **Ko** Kohli

VICTOR TRUMPER

(Australia)

George Beldam's famous photograph of Victor Trumper with his bat raised, striding out to meet the unseen ball, is one of cricket's most iconic images. Trumper was Australia's greatest batsman before the emergence of Don Bradman. 'Trumper at the zenith of his fame challenged comparison with Ranjitsinhji,' said *Wisden* in his obituary following his death in 1915. His first Test match – against England at Nottingham in 1899 – was W. G. Grace's last. In his next Test at Lord's, he scored a brilliant 135 not out in a ten-wicket victory for Australia. When he returned to the dressing room, he was told: 'There's a huge, bearded chap at the door demanding to see you, sir.' It was Grace, holding the bat he had used in his final Test at Nottingham. He handed the bat to Trumper. It was inscribed: 'From the past champion to the future champion.' Later on that tour, Trumper made his career best, 300 not out against Sussex, with Ranji and C. B. Fry (who made 181) on the opposition.

Trumper was renowned as a great player on difficult pitches. When he returned to England in 1902 he played one of the finest Ashes innings. In a low-scoring match at Manchester, which Australia won to set up a 2-0 lead with two Tests to play, he made 104 in under two hours 'without making a mistake of any kind', according to *Wisden*. 'His pulling was a marvel of ease and certainty.' He died from kidney disease aged only thirty-seven in 1915, just three years after his last Test.

BARRY RICHARDS

(South Africa)

He played only one Test series but it was enough to offer proof of his exceptional talent. It was Barry Richards's misfortune to have his international career cut short by South Africa's sporting isolation because of his government's apartheid policy. In cricket, the isolation lasted a generation and the tall, elegant, right-handed opener had to find other avenues to showcase his skills.

Those four matches against Australia in 1969–70 were South Africa's last officially sanctioned Tests for twenty-two years but they still resonate. South Africa's touring opponents, an impressive side wearied from a tour of India, were hammered 4-0 and Richards played his part. In the second Test at Durban, Richards made the first of two centuries in the series. South Africa's finest batsman, Graeme Pollock, stole the headlines with 274 but Richards's 140, made from 164 balls, was described by *Wisden* as 'technical perfection' while 'his only false stroke … was his last one'. Overall he made 508 runs at an average of 72 but for the rest of his eighteen-year career he had to make do with tearing up domestic cricket around the world.

From 1968 to 1976, playing for Hampshire in English county cricket, he was in the top twenty of the national batting averages every season. His top score was 356 for South Australia against a Western Australia attack including Dennis Lillee. He made 325 of those runs in a single day. For an opener to bat through an entire team innings is a rarity but he did it three times. Even rarer is to score a century in the two-hour session before lunch – Richards did it nine times.

BRENDON McCULLUM

(New Zealand)

After Australia had beaten New Zealand in the 2015 World Cup final, their flinty wicket-keeper Brad Haddin was asked to justify the verbal 'send-offs' given to Kiwi batsmen when they were dismissed. 'You know what? They deserved it,' said Haddin. 'They were that nice to us in New Zealand and we were that uncomfortable. I said in the team meeting: "I can't stand for this anymore, we're going at them as hard as we can."'

That niceness was largely the embodiment of the New Zealand captain Brendon McCullum. He could properly be categorised as an aggressor or possibly as an innovator. But taking all into account, he is the ultimate modern cricketing entertainer who has breathed fresh, minty air into a sometimes cynical, introspective world. When he brought his 'Black Caps' to England in 2015, New Zealand were cast as the *hors d'oeuvres* before the late-summer Ashes. Yet they played with such uninhibited vigour that not only did crowds fall in love with them and McCullum in particular, but the hard-pressed England team, trying to find themselves again after a bad year, were swept along too. Their wretchedly conservative one-day side reinvented itself overnight, essentially in McCullum's image. England went on to win the Ashes, against the odds, by playing aggressively and fearlessly.

McCullum was a wicket-keeper once but having become captain in 2012, he left the gloves at home preferring to dive headlong around the field in the manner of his All Black rugby equivalent, the demi-god Richie McCaw. In 2014 he became the first Kiwi to score a Test triple hundred. He batted for five minutes shy of thirteen hours to salvage an unlikely draw against India and thus secure a series victory. For the first time in a generation New Zealand had won two Test series in a home summer. That innings showed his versatility because in the short formats he opens the batting with an almost crazed, swing-from-the-hip attitude. In the first match of the inaugural Indian Premier League in 2008, he smashed thirteen sixes in an astonishing innings of 158 not out from seventy-three balls for Kolkata. In 2010 he became only the second batsman to score a century in a Twenty20 international.

WALLY HAMMOND

(England)

Imposing and majestic, Wally Hammond was England's answer to Don Bradman. Yet he was condemned to inhabit the shadow of the legendary Australian, an affliction that 'gnawed away at the surprisingly sensitive and fragile persona of Hammond', according to his biographer David Foot in *The Reasons Why*. His powerful elegance was in contrast to The Don's cold-blooded, ravenous run-scoring. 'I preferred to see just an hour of Walter Hammond to eight or ten hours of Don Bradman,' said Len Hutton. When Hammond died in 1966, Neville Cardus described him as, 'Cricket *in excelsis*'.

On only his second England tour, to Australia in 1928–29, he scored 905 runs at an average of 113, including double centuries in successive Tests at Sydney and Melbourne. It remains an English record run haul for an Ashes series and overall is bettered only, inevitably, by Bradman. At Auckland in 1933, he scored 336 not out against New Zealand in just over five hours. For five years until Len Hutton broke it, it was Test cricket's highest ever score.

Curiously, Hammond was more prolific overseas than at home, averaging sixty-six abroad to 'only' fifty in England. But one of his greatest innings came at Lord's in 1938 against Australia: scoring 240 to rescue England after they slipped to thirty-one for three on the first morning. 'There was no palpable effort,' wrote Cardus, 'no undignified outbursts of violence. It was a majestic innings, all the red-carpeted way to 240.' Hammond was also a very useful medium-pace bowler and an outstanding slip fielder where his 'lithe omnipresence has not often been equalled', according to Cardus.

29   E

Cm

Compton

DENIS COMPTON

(England)

No cricketer summed up the post-war spirit of renewal and resurgence in Britain better than Denis Compton. He was a right-handed batsman of daring, flair and flourish and also a footballer good enough to play for Arsenal in the 1950 FA Cup final. He was the Brylcreem Boy: one of the first British sportsmen, and certainly the first cricketer, to become a national celebrity in the modern sense with an off-field personality. And he had plenty of personality. It was not unknown for him to turn up in the morning at Lord's, where he played with such distinction for Middlesex, still wearing his dinner suit from the night before.

Growing up in north London, Compton made early impressions on important judges at Lord's and was on the staff at Lord's by the time he was fifteen. He made his Test debut in the same 1937 series against New Zealand as Len Hutton. Two more contrasting batsmen and characters one would not imagine. Both were heroic figures but in entirely different ways. In 1947, as Britain picked itself up after the war, Compton and his Middlesex batting partner Bill Edrich enjoyed the most golden summer of all. Compton scored 3,816 runs for Middlesex and England, including eighteen centuries. Both are records for an English season that still stand.

His friendly rivalry with the Australian all-rounder Keith Miller, whose carefree attitude to life and cricket chimed with Compton's, was an uplifting narrative of post-war Ashes matches. It was Compton who hit the winning runs for England at The Oval to reclaim the Ashes in 1953.

GRAEME POLLOCK

(South Africa)

After making 127 not out at Perth on his first tour with South Africa in 1963–64, Don Bradman approached Graeme Pollock and said: 'If you ever score a century like that again I hope I'm there to see it.' He did, often. Although not as often for his country as he and his supporters would have liked. Pollock's Test career was cut short after twenty-three matches by South Africa's sporting isolation but not before he had scored seven centuries and averaged 60.97, the second highest career average after Bradman for those who have had more than twenty innings.

A schoolboy prodigy, Pollock was a left-hander with power and timing who became, at sixteen, the youngest batsman to score a century in South Africa's domestic Currie Cup competition. At nineteen, he became the youngest South African to score a first-class double century. When he was twenty-eight he was the youngest man to pass 1,000 runs in Test cricket. His most memorable innings was his 274 against Australia at Durban in 1970 when he and Barry Richards destroyed the tourists' attack. 'He attacked continuously and with merciless efficiency,' reported *Wisden*. The innings contained forty-three boundaries and remained South Africa's highest Test score for twenty-nine years.

ZAHEER ABBAS

(Pakistan)

'A bespectacled, bookish-looking batsman unleashing cover drive after wristy cover drive,' is how Kamran Abbasi, on ESPNcricinfo, described Zaheer Abbas, a Pakistan great and the first Asian batsman to score a hundred first-class centuries. A tall right-hander, he was predominantly a front-foot player, something which served him especially well during thirteen seasons with Gloucestershire in English county cricket where he became a cult figure, known affectionately as Zed. Four times for the county, Zaheer scored a double century and a century in the same match – a first-class record – and was not out on each occasion. He also holds the joint record with Ricky Ponting for scoring a century in each innings of a match, a feat he achieved eight times.

Four of his twelve three-figure scores in Test matches were double hundreds, one of the best conversion rates in history. In only his third innings, against England at Birmingham in 1971, he made his highest Test score, 274. 'One soon appreciated that he was a batsman out of the ordinary,' said *Wisden*. Eleven years later, against India at Lahore, he reached his hundredth first-class century with 215, an innings he followed up with 186 and 168 in his next two innings of the series.

GREG CHAPPELL

(Australia)

An intriguing and unusual combination of elegance allied to self-discipline, Greg Chappell was one of three brothers to play for Australia and the cornerstone of the nation's batting line-up through the 1970s and early 1980s. His personality and demeanour could not have been more different to his older brother Ian, one of Australia's most successful captains and the hirsute embodiment of the boozy, blokeish and ballsy culture of Australian cricket in the 1970s.

Greg captained Australia too, though with mixed success and with less obvious aptitude for it. Infamously, in February 1981, he instructed his other brother, Trevor, to bowl the final delivery of a one-day international against New Zealand underarm, in order to deny the opposition even a sniff of scoring the six they needed to tie the match. It was a practice that has since been outlawed and was condemned instantly by all observers, including Ian Chappell who happened to commentating for Channel 9 television at the time.

'A tall, slim, lean man – even a little austere,' wrote Gideon Haigh. He did not exude style when he stood at the crease, with his shirtsleeves buttoned to the wrists. But when he unleashed a cover drive or a flick through the leg side, one was left in no doubt as to his qualities. He made a century on his Test debut in 1970, batting at number seven, and made his twenty-second in his final Test in 1984, when he, Dennis Lillee and Rod Marsh – three pillars of Australian cricket – all retired at once. Some of his most impressive batting was in the 'Supertests' of Kerry Packer's breakaway World Series Cricket in 1979: Chappell made 620 runs at an average of 69 in five Supertests in the Caribbean against a West Indies bowling attack of exceptional pace and hostility.

DAVID GOWER

(England)

It took a single delivery for the twenty-one-year-old, flaxen-haired left-hander to confirm the promise that the unusually bold England selectors had invested in him in 1978. The ease with which Gower pulled his first ball in Test cricket for four, from Liaquat Ali of Pakistan, was 'one of the most auspicious beginnings in recent years', reported *Wisden*. The little yellow book wasn't wrong: Gower went on to become England's leading Test run-scorer, before Graham Gooch overtook him, and he did so with a jaw-dropping nonchalance. His timing was exquisite, his hand-eye co-ordination so sharp that some of his best innings came against the express pace of the 1980s West Indies.

Gower could play the long innings too but mostly he adhered to his natural stroke-making style, which made him as frustrating a batsman as he was entertaining. He had two shots at the England captaincy, both of which ended in humiliation, once at the hands of West Indies and then against Australia. In among the wreckage he had the glorious summer of 1985 when the Ashes were regained and Gower scored three centuries in five innings to finish the series with 732 runs, the most by an England batsman in a home Ashes series. In retirement, Gower has been an understated and insouciant TV presenter while continuing to indulge his well-publicised love of fine wine.

Column 6

25 A **Tr** Trumper		**42** E **Fr** Fry
26 SA **Rb** B. Richards	**34** NZ **Cw** Crowe	**43** SA **Dv** de Villiers
27 NZ **Mc** McCullum	**35** I **T** Tendulkar	**44** A **Ml** Miller
28 E **Hm** Hammond	**36** WI **Lr** Lara	**45** P **Im** Imran
29 E **Cm** Compton	**37** A **Wm** M. Waugh	**46** I **Kd** Kapil Dev
30 SA **Pg** G. Pollock	**38** A **Pn** Ponting	**47** E **Am** Ames
31 P **Z** Zaheer	**39** A **Cl** Clarke	**48** E **Kn** Knott
32 A **Cg** G. Chappell	**40** SL **Sg** Sangakkara	**49** I **Bd** Bedi
33 E **Gw** Gower	**41** I **Ko** Kohli	**50** E **An** Anderson

MARTIN CROWE

(New Zealand)

In the 1980s, New Zealand punched above their weight thanks almost exclusively to the talents of Richard Hadlee with the ball and Martin Crowe with the bat. With his father Dave a first-class cricketer, his brother Jeff also a New Zealand Test player and his mother Audrey a talented all-round sportswoman, Martin always seemed destined for a cricketing career. You may have heard of his cousin Russell, the film star.

He made his debut at nineteen but had to wait two years to make his first century. He made sixteen more Test centuries, the most by a New Zealand batsman, and had a conversion rate of fifties to hundreds of almost fifty per cent. His style was classical and conventional but notable for the amount of time he seemingly had to play his shots. Of his century against England at Lord's in 1986, *Wisden* asserted: 'Crowe's range of strokes ... showed ... that he had entered the ranks of world-class batsmen.'

Crowe reserved some of his best innings for New Zealand's trans-Tasman rivalry with Australia. He averaged a shade under sixty-seven in Australia and made 188 during the famous victory at Brisbane in 1985 that kicked off New Zealand's first series win over Australia (Hadlee taking nine wickets in an innings). In the first match of the 1992 World Cup against co-hosts Australia, he scored an unbeaten century with a knee injury and then showed initiative as captain by opening the bowling with a spinner. He was a man ahead of his time, as also shown by his attempt to launch Cricket Max, a scaled-down version of the game that, while never successful, predated the emergence of Twenty20.

SACHIN TENDULKAR

(India)

On 24 February 2010, Sachin Tendulkar almost broke the Internet. As he moved towards the first double century ever scored in a one-day international, the servers bearing the weight of the traffic to ESPNcricinfo, the world's biggest cricket website, started to bend. 'Among other things, he also broke a couple of our servers that day,' wrote ESPNcricinfo's global editor Sambit Bal. The match report for that game – a run-of-the-mill one-dayer against South Africa at the north Indian cricketing outpost of Gwalior – received forty-five million page views.

Greatness was expected of Tendulkar even before he and a friend, Vinod Kambli, put on 664 in a match for their school in Mumbai. He made his Test debut at sixteen in Pakistan, when he was hit in the mouth by the pace bowler Waqar Younis; he scored his maiden hundred at seventeen to save a Test in England; and at ninteen made a century on the world's fastest pitch in Perth against a fine Australian attack. Compact and well-balanced at the crease, he seemed to have no obvious weaknesses. Over time, like so many other great players, he adapted his game, becoming more restrained in order to feed the vast expectation on him every time he walked out to bat. He had no privacy in India, forced into indulging his passion for fast cars in the middle of the Mumbai night or wearing a disguise to go to the cinema.

Tendulkar dabbled in captaincy but it was never his thing: he just wanted to bat. The last phase of his career finished in the fraught and drawn-out pursuit of a hundred international hundreds, a unique feat he reached in his penultimate one-dayer against Bangladesh in 2012. A year earlier had been the true culmination of this phenomenal cricketing story when India lifted the World Cup, the first side to do so on home soil.

He holds a host of batting records: he has scored more Test and ODI runs than anyone in history, likewise more centuries in both formats. His haul of forty-nine ODI hundreds is nineteen more than the next man on the list. Across all international formats, he scored 34,357 runs (6,000 more than his nearest rival, Kumar Sangakkara), including those 100 hundreds and 164 fifties.

BRIAN LARA

(West Indies)

'All I wanna ask is, did I entertain?' asked a smiling Brian Lara of the crowd at Kensington Oval in Barbados, after his last match for the West Indies in the 2007 World Cup. The huge cheer that rang round the ground told him all he needed to know. The left-handed Trinidadian was a rare combination of extravagant flair, infuriating unpredictability and an unquenchable thirst for run-making.

At his best, it seemed that if Lara set his mind to it, he could not be dismissed. His first Test century was 277 and his third, in Antigua in 1994, was a new world Test record score: 375, beating Sir Garfield Sobers's mark of 365 set in 1958. A few weeks later, he broke the overall first-class record, amassing an eye-watering 501 not out for Warwickshire against Durham. When the Australian Matthew Hayden trumped the Test record with 380 in 2003, it took Lara only 185 days to raise the bar again, making 400 not out, again in Antigua, and again against England. The difference this time, though, was that England had already wrapped up a 3-0 series win.

And that was the burden Lara had to bear for much of his career, that of carrying – either figuratively or literally as captain – a proud cricketing territory that was in steep decline. When he retired from Tests in 2006 he had lost more matches (sixty-three) than any player in history, a record since claimed by Shiv Chanderpaul.

But he had a special ability to win Test matches on his own, never better exemplified than in the home series against a top Australian side in 1999. After the West Indies were dispatched with ease in the first Test,

Lara responded with 213 in the second, in a match containing only three others scores above 50. In the third Test in Barbados, with the score 1-1, Lara produced perhaps his greatest performance. West Indies conceded a 161-run deficit and appeared never to be in the hunt for their second-innings pursuit of 308 to win. They were 105 for five, 248 for eight and 302 for nine. But Lara repelled the Australian bowlers by himself until he lashed Jason Gillespie through the covers for the boundary that gave West Indies a one-wicket victory. No other batsman scored more than thirty-eight in the innings. Lara's performance was 'another transcendent innings', purred *Wisden*, and 'the hand of genius'.

MARK WAUGH

(Australia)

The younger twin of Steve Waugh by a few minutes, Mark Waugh was known as Junior throughout his career, and also, less kindly, as Afghan – the forgotten Waugh. But there was nothing forgettable about his batting. So sumptuous was his on-driving – restrained, balanced and perfectly timed – that it is easy to overlook his ability to score runs all round the wicket. Mark had to wait five years after his brother's debut to play his first Test for Australia, against England at Adelaide in January 1991, when he actually replaced Steve in the side. 'It proved to be the perfect combination – picturesque ground and glorious on-side stroke-making,' said Ian Chappell, the former Australia captain turned TV commentator. Waugh's first scoring stroke was a gentle, languid straight drive and he never looked back.

He could send the ball into the crowd with the best of them but he never appeared to be hitting the ball hard. Waugh would often lose his wicket for inexplicable reasons, conforming almost to the 'flawed genius' stereotype. His overall Test record – 8,029 runs at forty-one, with a highest score of 153 not out – suffers by comparison with the other Australian batsmen of that era of global domination. But for spectators who saw him live or watched on television, the privilege was all theirs. He had a formidable one-day record too, including three centuries in the 1996 World Cup when Australia were runners-up and a then-record score by an Australian, 173, against West Indies at Melbourne in 2001. An enigmatic, slightly aloof character, eyes often hidden behind sunglasses, Waugh was also a superb slip fielder. When he played his last Test in 2002 he had taken more catches (181) than any non-wicket-keeper in history.

38	A
Pn	
Ponting	

RICKY PONTING

(Australia)

The Ricky Ponting pull shot was a mixture of beauty and brutality but entirely his own, a signature dish to savour. The first movement was forward and then, if the ball was even a touch too short, he rocked back, extended his thick, hairy forearms and cracked the ball with the sound of gunshot through midwicket, all while remaining perfectly balanced as he pivoted round on his right foot.

At his best, from the late 1990s to the mid 2000s, Ponting was impossible to bowl to: to counter the pull shot, bowlers would pitch the ball fuller and watch a powerful, assertive straight drive send it back past them to the boundary. Expectations were always considerable on Ponting, right from when this slight youth from Tasmania debuted in 1996. He had to overcome several hurdles in his early career: a black eye from a fight in a Sydney bar led to a public dressing down and a reassessment of his goals. His nickname of Punter told of his love of gambling and greyhound racing. But marriage in 2002 grounded Ponting and prefaced a remarkable eighteen-month period in which he scored ten Test centuries against five different nations and, as captain, scored a match-winning 140 not out in the final of the 2003 World Cup.

It was his curse that he was almost the last man standing when the world-beating Australian side of that era broke up. But credit to Ponting's resilience and determination: he did not quit but continued to lead Australia through periods of turbulence and transition. His 156 at Manchester in the epic 2005 Ashes single-handedly saved Australia from defeat, though his side ultimately conceded the series. In 2010–11 he became the only Australian to captain three Ashes-losing teams. He retired in 2012 as the second leading Test run-scorer of all time behind Sachin Tendulkar.

39   A

Cl

Clarke

MICHAEL CLARKE

(Australia)

Blond highlights, tattoos and a celebrity lifestyle didn't fit every Australian's idea of what a leading cricketer, and potential captain, should look like. But Michael Clarke deflected the slings and arrows of public opinion to become one of his country's leading run-scorers: 8,643 in Tests and nine shy of 8,000 in one-dayers. He retired in 2015 after an emotionally and physically draining tour of England – a trip too far for his ailing body – in which the Ashes were lost ignominiously. He often seemed to be a man apart from his team and, as such, his leadership was often questioned but his imaginative tactics and innovative field-placings won him plenty of fans at home and abroad. And in early 2015, he led his side to victory in their home World Cup and was Australia's top scorer in the final.

A slight man, with huge drive and ambition, Clarke was a deft batsman with a classy cover drive and a delicate cut shot. He had a phenomenal maiden series in India in 2004. He made 151 on his Test debut at Bangalore and three Tests later bowled Australia to what should have been a winning position at Mumbai when he took six for nine with his left-arm spin. Over time a worsening back condition prevented him bowling and indeed affected his batting too. He remained an outstanding slip fielder and razor sharp anywhere close to the wicket.

In 2011 he took over Australia's Test captaincy from Ricky Ponting following home defeat in the Ashes. In 2012 he scored almost 1,600 Test runs including an unbeaten 329 against India on his home ground at Sydney. The following year, having lost the Ashes in England, he led Australia to a 5-0 clean sweep of their oldest rivals in home turf, their first victory in four Ashes series. Two months later he played one of the game's bravest innings, 161 not out with a broken shoulder against a South African pace barrage at Cape Town. In late 2014, Clarke gained new respect for his statesmanlike response to the death of his friend and teammate Phillip Hughes, who never recovered after being hit on the head by the ball while batting.

KUMAR SANGAKKARA

(Sri Lanka)

Good-looking, articulate and stylishly prolific in all formats of the game, Kumar Sangakkara established his place in his late thirties as a modern cricketing great, with achievements that stretch beyond the field of play. His speech at Lord's in 2011 (the annual Cowdrey Lecture) about the parlous state of cricket administration in his native Sri Lanka and around the world was brave, memorable and important, especially coming from a current player.

Sangakarra was a law student when he first played, as a wicket-keeper/batsman, for Sri Lanka at the age of twenty-two in late 2000. A few months later he was sledging England's veteran captain Mike Atherton from behind the stumps, indicating a feistiness that has since been subsumed by a more magisterial demeanour. He was a batsman in the best traditions of elegant left-handedness with a well-balanced cover drive to die for. When he gave up the keeping gloves for good in Test matches in 2008, his batting just got better and better.

Sangakarra established a joyfully irresistible middle-order partnership with his great friend, and business partner, Mahela Jayawardene, a right-hander of beautifully understated class, who has a strong case to be in this table as well. The pair were the bedrock of Sri Lankan batting for the best part of fifteen years and took their side to the World Cup final of 2011 where, despite Jayawardene's astoundingly good century, they lost to India. In the 2015 World Cup in Australia, Sangakkara scored a record four hundreds in successive innings. He retired from internationals in August 2015 as the second leading one-day run-scorer of all time, one of five men to have passed 12,000 Test runs and second only to Don Bradman with eleven Test scores of 200 or more.

VIRAT KOHLI

(India)

Every inch the contemporary cricketer, Virat Kohli embodies the new India. By late 2015, he had played more than four times as many one-day internationals as he had Test matches and scored twice as many centuries in the fifty-over form as he had in the five-day game. 'Indian cricketer, gamer, car lover, loves soccer and an enthusiast,' reads the profile for his Twitter account, which has more than eight million followers.

His personal life is as likely to be a cause of media attention as his batting exploits and that says more about the status of India's cricketers than it does his off-field habits. Though criticised in his early days for being too brash, he has matured to a point where he took over the Test captaincy from M. S. Dhoni in late 2014. His first match was an emotionally charged affair at Adelaide immediately following the shocking death of Australian batsman Phillip Hughes a few weeks earlier. Kohli not only made a dashing century in each innings of the Test but earned universal admiration for his pursuit of the victory target, rather than settling for a draw. India lost by forty-eight runs but Kohli said afterwards: 'No regrets. This is what we play cricket for.'

'Kohli is fulfilling a prime task for a captain by making the cricket interesting for his players,' wrote Ian Chappell, the former Australian skipper on ESPNcricinfo, while making the point that Kohli is part of a new generation of international captains who are heavily influenced by the attacking mindset of Twenty20. By his twenty-seventh birthday, in November 2015, Kohli had twenty-three ODI centuries, joint-fifth on the all-time list. Two of those centuries have come in India's opening matches of the two World Cup tournaments he has played in – 2011, when he helped India to the title, and 2015.

Column 7

	42 E **Fr** Fry	
34 NZ **Cw** Crowe	**43** SA **Dv** de Villiers	**51** E **Br** Brearley
35 I **T** Tendulkar	**44** A **Ml** Miller	**52** WI **Gl** Gayle
36 WI **Lr** Lara	**45** P **Im** Imran	**53** E **Jd** Jardine
37 A **Wm** M. Waugh	**46** I **Kd** Kapil Dev	**54** P **Mn** Miandad
38 A **Pn** Ponting	**47** E **Am** Ames	**55** P **Iz** Inzamam-ul-Haq
39 A **Cl** Clarke	**48** E **Kn** Knott	**56** E **Ce** Close
40 SL **Sg** Sangakkara	**49** I **Bd** Bedi	**57** E **Gr** Greig
41 I **Ko** Kohli	**50** E **An** Anderson	**58** E **Pt** Pietersen

C. B. FRY

(England)

In cricket the all-rounder is a versatile beast but there has never been an all-rounder quite like C. B. Fry. He wasn't an all-rounder in cricket terms because he was essentially a batsman – and a very fine one – but the range of his other successes is remarkable. In addition to cricketing brilliance, he equalled the world long-jump record and played football for England and for Southampton in the 1902 FA Cup final. He was also a writer, diplomat and politician. 'I think there are politicians and actors and KCs [King's Counsel] and authors enough. There has only been one C. B. Fry,' wrote Neville Cardus. His off-field accomplishments did lead to tall tales, such as the apocryphal story that he had once been offered the throne of Albania.

Fry's approach to batting was almost scientific and to watch him and Ranji in full flow for Sussex was to witness a perfect pair of complementary opposites. Unlike Ranji, who liked to play off the back foot, Fry was known for his straight driving off the front foot. He averaged 50 in first-class cricket with more than 30,000 runs, although his Test career was not as prolific as his talent suggested it should be. He made two Test centuries, both at The Oval. His first and greater of the two (144) came against Australia in his fourteenth Test in 1905. 'For the first time in a Test match, the famous batsman did himself full justice,' reported *Wisden*. His greatest season was 1901 when he made 3,147 runs and scored six centuries in succession, a record only by Don Bradman and Mike Procter.

A. B. DE VILLIERS

(South Africa)

'I decided when I was ten that I was going to do something in sport one day,' says A. B. de Villiers on his own website with the insouciance that only a man of such immense, wide-ranging talents can possess. He could have played fly-half for the Blue Bulls, the rugby team of his home territory in Pretoria; he was in the national tennis squad; and he has played golf off scratch. But cricket has been his calling and the game should be grateful he made that choice. South Africa certainly are. He is a phenomenal batting talent across all formats of the game, a wicket-keeper and an outstanding fielder maintaining the standards set by Jonty Rhodes back in the 1990s.

Despite his talents and the accolades, de Villiers is not a big shot, but is impressively and endearingly humble. By late 2015, after a decade in the game, he was still only thirty-one and seemingly has many worlds still to conquer: averaging more than fifty in both Tests and one-dayers and with twenty-one centuries in both formats. In limited-overs cricket, he has the poise to move around the crease and the hand-eye co-ordination to play outrageously unlikely shots all around the wicket. In Tests, he has the technical rigour and concentration to play the long innings, as he showed early in his career with a nine-hour unbeaten 178 against West Indies in Barbados. He also made South Africa's first ever double century against India at Ahmedabad in 2008.

KEITH MILLER

(Australia)

Having been a fighter pilot in the Second World War, Keith Miller was not about to let the intensity of international cricket get on top of him: 'Pressure is a Messerschmitt up your arse,' was one of the Australian all-rounder's more famous quotes. But that should not disguise his natural competitiveness. A hard-hitting attacking batsman, Miller was also a seriously quick bowler and was even barracked at Nottingham in the first Test of the 1948 Ashes when he over-used the bouncer. Fundamentally, though, he played the game for fun with a smile on his face. It was a face, coupled with the slick quiff, that melted a thousand hearts. 'There has never been a more glamorous cricketer,' wrote historian David Frith. When in England, he was a regular at Royal Ascot, adorning the newspapers in top hat and tails, hob-nobbing with celebrities and royalty.

Miller started out as a batsman and as an eighteen-year-old hit 181 for Victoria against Tasmania. In 1945, he made a name for himself in the Victory Tests, blazing 185 at Lord's for The Dominions and sending one six into the top of the pavilion, a vast hit very rarely achieved. In the third Test of the 1950–51 series against England, which Australia won to retain the Ashes, Miller made a significant all-round contribution. On the first day, he took a blinding slip catch to dismiss Cyril Washbrook and took the next three wickets to fall. Then he made an unbeaten 145 to set up a winning first-innings lead for Australia. In his last Test at Lord's in 1956, aged thirty-six, he summoned his best bowling figures in a match – ten for 152 – in a victory on an otherwise disappointing tour. As he left the field, he picked the bails from the umpire's pocket and tossed them as souvenirs into the crowd.

IMRAN KHAN

(Pakistan)

Rarely has captaincy had such a positive effect on a cricketer as it did with Pakistan's finest, Imran Khan. Over time he reinvented – or refined – himself from modest pace bowler and aggressive batsman into a world-class all-rounder, World Cup-winning skipper and international celebrity. 'A shy, introspective mama's boy, he became cricket's James Bond, as smooth on the field as away from it,' wrote the Pakistani journalist Osman Samiuddin on ESPNcricinfo. The statistics alone provide a stark contrast. As captain in Test matches, he averaged fifty-two with the bat, as opposed to twenty-five when he wasn't. And with the ball he averaged only twenty against a still respectable twenty-five when he wasn't.

Born into an affluent Lahore family, his cousins Javed Burki and Majid Khan also played for Pakistan. They were Oxbridge-educated too and Imran also followed the same path, playing for Oxford University in the early 1970s, having already toured England with Pakistan. A rigorous schooling in the rebel World Series Cricket in Australia in the late 1970s helped inspire Imran to greater things. In full flow he was a majestic sight: dark mane flowing, his broad-chested, upright run to the crease culminated in a classical leap into the delivery stride.

He took on the captaincy of Pakistan in 1982 and after a first Test win at Lord's, produced an inspired, sustained series of fast bowling against India. His forty wickets in six Tests on pitches traditionally considered graveyards for the quicker bowlers gave Pakistan a 3-0 victory. In 1987 he led his side to their first series victory in England, taking ten wickets in the decisive win at Leeds. His greatest moment, though, was the 1992 World Cup final when Pakistan, after a terrible group stage when they were almost eliminated, defeated England at Melbourne to take the trophy for the first time. After cricket, his marriage to, and subsequent split from, Jemima Goldsmith was a source of British tabloid interest while he swam the shark-infested waters of Pakistani politics.

KAPIL DEV

(India)

Bowling fast on the mostly slow pitches of India has generally been a thankless task, hence the tradition of spin bowling for which the nation has been so renowned. Kapil Dev bucked the trend. An athletic artist with the ball, and a cavalier with the bat, he took his place in a rare pantheon of world-class all-rounders in the 1980s, alongside Richard Hadlee, Ian Botham and Imran Khan. 'Charming but deadly,' wrote Mike Selvey in *Wisden*. His longevity – 131 Tests over more than fifteen years – was testament to his strength and stamina. He was the leading Test wicket-taker for sixteen years until Courtney Walsh passed his mark of 434 in 2000. And he scored more than 5,000 highly entertaining Test-match runs, including one sequence at Lord's in 1990 when he saved the follow-on for India with four successive sixes.

Kapil Dev's most memorable achievements came in the one-day arena, and specifically the 1983 World Cup in England. In a group match against unfancied Zimbabwe, at the cutesy but small-time venue of Tunbridge Wells, India were seventeen for five, and primed for an embarrassing upset. But Kapil unleashed one of the great limited-overs innings: 175 not out from 138 balls with sixteen fours and six sixes. He had never made a one-day century before and, as it happened, would never do so again but this was the highest score ever made in the format. As a career highlight, it was bettered only by what was to occur a week later at Lord's in the final. Facing the might of West Indies, who had won the first two World Cup tournaments, India appeared not to have set their hot-shot opponents a large enough target (184 to get in sixty overs). Kapil, the captain, played a key part in the stunning demise of the champions. When Viv Richards top-edged a pull off medium-pacer Madan Lal, Kapil ran back from square leg and made a very difficult, over-the-shoulder catch look remarkably easy. West Indies collapsed, victims of their own complacency and India's unbreakable spirit. It was a result that changed cricket – the television age was dawning in India, whose vast population would display an apparently limitless appetite for the game and turn their country into a global commercial powerhouse.

LES AMES

(England)

Les Ames was the game's first great wicket-keeper/
batsman, a combination of skills that is now taken as a
prerequisite for modern glovemen. Bubbly and energetic,
Ames was England's first-choice keeper for most of the
1930s, including on the Bodyline tour of 1932–33 when he
was keeping to some of the quickest bowling – from Harold
Larwood and Bill Voce – ever seen. He used to cushion the
blows by placing slices of steak inside the gloves. Keeping
to the spinners, he was unobtrusively efficient.

There might conceivably have been better wicket-
keepers around – though that is a moot point – but
Ames's batting gave him a definite edge. He averaged
forty in Test cricket and made 102 first-class centuries
through a twenty-five-year career that was interrupted
by the Second World War. He remains the most prolific
keeper-batsman in first-class history with 37,248 runs and
three times he scored 1,000 runs and made 100 dismissals
in an English season. One of his most significant
innings came at Lord's in 1934 against Australia, a
match that came to be defined by the fourteen wickets
taken by spinner Hedley Verity. Ames made 120 and, in
conjunction with Maurice Leyland, elevated England's
first innings from 182 for five to 440 all out. That set up
England's first Test victory over Australia at Lord's since
1896 and, as it turned out, their last until 2009.

ALAN KNOTT

(England)

'An impish genius', according to the writer and
broadcaster Christopher Martin-Jenkins, Alan Knott was
England's wicket-keeper in eighty-nine of ninety-three
Tests from his debut in 1967 up to the World Series
Cricket breakaway in 1977, of which he was a part.

All the best wicket-keepers who stand the test of time develop a winning partnership with a particular bowler and Knott was no exception. His telepathic understanding with his Kent teammate Derek Underwood was one of the joys of English cricket for more than a decade, through the late 1960s right up to the early 1980s. For much of that time Underwood, a left-arm spinner whose stock delivery was medium pace rather than slow, was bowling on pitches that were left open to the elements during the course of a match. On a damp or drying surface, he could be unplayable, which also presented a significant challenge to Knott, who would stand up to the stumps and catch cleanly whatever devilish delivery that 'Deadly' managed to make lift or spit off the pitch.

Short and slight, Knott was distinguishable by his mop of dark hair, usually covered by a small sun hat or cap, piercing dark eyes, his trademark red gloves and sleeves buttoned to the wrists. He was stylish and mildly eccentric too. He was a highly competent and inventive middle-order batsman who scored five Test centuries for England. And he could adapt his style accordingly: at Adelaide in the bruising 1974–75 Ashes defeat he made a battling 106 not out in a losing cause while at Trent Bridge in 1977, also against Australia, he made an attacking 135 – his last Test hundred – to set up an England victory.

BISHAN BEDI

(India)

By the time he had played his last Test in 1979, Bishan Singh Bedi was India's leading wicket-taker. But that really is only part of the story. 'The first epithet that comes to mind for Bishan Bedi's bowling is "beautiful",' wrote the former England captain Mike Brearley in *Wisden*. Bedi was a left-arm spinner in the classical tradition. Fizzing the ball from hand to hand in readiness to bowl, he would approach the wicket with a rhythmic, side-on action. His variations were subtle, an extra tweak of the fingers here, an adjustment of the wrist there. 'Of all the slow bowlers of Bedi's time, none forced you to commit yourself later than he did,' added Brearley.

Bedi was one of the architects of India's death-by-spin strategy of the late 1960s and 1970s. There were two, three and sometimes four twirlers in India's line-up, all offering different challenges for the batsman. There was the master of flight, off-spinner Erapalli Prasanna; the leg-spinner with the left-arm withered by childhood polio, Bhagwath Chandrasekhar; and the more orthodox off-spinner, Srinivasaraghavan Venkataraghavan. He was also renowned for having a big heart, which was never better exemplified than when he took his best Test figures. In a losing cause against Australia at Kolkata in 1969, he bowled fifty overs and took seven for ninety-eight while Prasanna bowled forty-nine wicketless overs at the other end.

He was always a feisty competitor and in retirement offered outspoken opinions on the game, particularly the thorny issue of legal bowling actions. He was a harsh critic of the Sri Lankan legend Muttiah Muralitharan.

JAMES ANDERSON

(England)

A starlet at twenty and a bona fide star a decade later, James Anderson was the millennial successor to Fred Trueman as England's king of swing, although in style he is more akin to Trueman's great new-ball partner, Brian Statham. In 2015 he became England's leading Test wicket-taker, a record once held by Trueman, and the country's first bowler to 400 wickets. He is not as quick as the South African Dale Steyn but there has been no more skilful exponent of swing than Anderson.

His rise was rapid and unexpected. He had only just broken into the Lancashire team when he found himself in England's World Cup side in early 2003. His superb burst of four for twenty-nine against Pakistan at Cape Town, including two wickets in two balls, confirmed a special talent. But it took a while for this diffident character to fulfil his undoubted potential. Various attempts to refine his natural bowling action (that involved the quirk of his head pointing at the ground while delivering the ball) only served to confuse and frustrate.

In 2008, as England's ageing bowling attack from the 2005 Ashes was being disbanded, Anderson's time came. Over the next half-dozen seasons, he would become a global force and unplayable in home conditions. He honed the rare ability of being able to swing the ball both ways, without obviously telegraphing the change to the batsman. He worked out ways to be effective when the ball wasn't swinging conventionally. His part in England's historic series win in Australia in 2010–11 was a special triumph for Anderson (twenty-four wickets at twenty-six runs each) because he had had such a torrid time on the previous tour in 2006–07.

Over time his natural shyness, often misinterpreted as surliness, has given way to a dry, understated wit and a public popularity to complement his on-field success.

Mavericks
& Rebels

Cricket takes all sorts. Despite often being hidebound by convention and tradition – or perhaps because of it – dressing rooms at every level of the game, all over the world, have fostered the full range of human qualities and frailties.

The over-confident, the insecure, doers, thinkers, diplomats, agitators, altruists and individualists all find a place in a cricket team. 'It's not easy being me in that dressing room,' Kevin Pietersen, one of our Mavericks & Rebels, memorably said in 2012 – sowing a cryptic seed about rifts within the England team that were in full bloom more than a year later.

Column 8

42 E **Fr** Fry	
43 SA **Dv** de Villiers	**51** E **Br** Brearley
44 A **Ml** Miller	**52** WI **Gl** Gayle
45 P **Im** Imran	**53** E **Jd** Jardine
46 I **Kd** Kapil Dev	**54** P **Mn** Miandad
47 E **Am** Ames	**55** P **Iz** Inzamam-ul-Haq
48 E **Kn** Knott	**56** E **Ce** Close
49 I **Bd** Bedi	**57** E **Gr** Greig
50 E **An** Anderson	**58** E **Pt** Pietersen	**59** SA **Cr** Cronje

MIKE BREARLEY

51	E
Br	
Brearley	

(England)

Lured away from life as a university lecturer to captain his county, Middlesex in 1971 and enticed out of retirement to skipper an ailing England side a decade later, Mike Brearley was the last of the 'specialist' captains. Even though he was a professional, he was a throwback to the days when teams in England were always captained by educated amateurs.

While he was a prolific county batsman, Brearley struggled at international level and never made a Test century. He had the good fortune never to captain against the all-conquering West Indies but his leadership, at domestic and Test level, was among the most intuitive, imaginative and successful the sport has ever seen. He once placed a protective helmet where he would normally have a fielder to entice the batsman to hit it and claim the five-run penalty incurred for a ball hitting a fielder's helmet, which is normally placed behind the wicket-keeper. Indeed the laws of the game were changed to outlaw this innovative practice.

Brearley was a supreme man-manager. He was described by *Wisden as* 'a master in the art of cricket' while Australian fast bowler Rodney Hogg had a cuter observation: 'He has a degree in people.' In a sense, as a trained and practising psychoanalyst, he does. He led England to Ashes victories in 1977 and 1978–79 but his finest hour came in 1981. Brearley had relinquished the England captaincy a year earlier but with England 1-0 down after two Tests, his replacement Ian Botham resigned. Asked who should be the new captain, Botham answered unequivocally that it should be Brearley. So it was, and what followed was one of the most remarkable turnarounds in cricket history with a reborn Botham, inspired and wanted by Brearley's paternalistic stewardship, leading England to a series of improbable victories.

52	WI
Gl	
Gayle	

CHRIS GAYLE

(West Indies)

'If u don't have a strip club at home, u ain't a cricket "player"', tweeted Chris Gayle while showing the online world one of the more bizarre domestic installations. The self-styled 'world boss' has taken the idea of cricketer as celebrity to new levels. A Jamaican left-handed opening batsman of exceptional timing and rare brutality, Gayle became a hero for the Twenty20 generation, combining implausibly fierce hitting with a swaggering cool. But he crossed the line in early 2016 when his behaviour towards a female interviewer on live television provoked a huge backlash and landed him with a fine.

His strength and bat-speed make him a nightmarish opponent at the start of an innings. He mastered all three formats of the game – his highest Test score is 333 and in 2015 he came the first man to score a double century in a World Cup – but Twenty20 has been his true calling.

Traversing the globe from the Indian Premier League to England's T20 Blast, Australia's Big Bash League and then back to the Caribbean, Gayle left a trail of demoralised bowlers and open-mouthed fans wherever he went. He illuminated the opening match of the inaugural World Twenty20 tournament in South Africa by scoring 117 from fifty-seven balls. By late 2015, he had scored more than 8,000 runs in all Twenty20 matches, 1,500 more than the next best. At the time of writing, he had scored sixteen T20 hundreds, nine more than Brendon McCullum, the other pre-eminent blaster of the age.

Just like his compatriot Usain Bolt in the sprint world, Gayle has continually raised the bar of limited-overs batsmanship. In 2013, he made 175 not out – the highest T20 score – for Royal Challengers Bangalore against Pune Warriors, reaching his hundred off only thirty balls. Allan Donald, the Pune coach, said his bowlers were 'scared' to bowl to Gayle. No wonder.

DOUGLAS JARDINE

(England)

With his aquiline nose, multi-coloured Harlequin cap and white neckerchief, Douglas Jardine encapsulated everything that Australians despised about English cricket and the 'mother country'. His career was defined by his captaincy of England in the 1932–33 Ashes series in Australia when his tactics – known as leg theory by supporters and 'Bodyline' by opponents – caused controversy and acrimony, escalating to a level where relations between Britain and Australia were strained to breaking point.

Appointed England captain in 1932, Jardine set about devising a way to stop Australia's batting phenomenon, Don Bradman. Bradman had been unstoppable in the 1930 Ashes but Jardine, and others, had noticed one perceived chink in Bradman's armour: that he had struggled against fast bowling on a damp pitch at The Oval. 'I've got it! He's yellow,' Jardine had exclaimed when he saw film of the relevant innings. So for the 1932 Ashes series in Australia, Jardine packed his side with fast bowlers, notably Harold Larwood, and instructed them to bowl at batsmen's bodies with an umbrella of fielders on the leg side waiting for catches.

The tactics were successful and England won the series 4-1. But batsmen were injured in the process and the vast Australian crowds turned on Jardine. At one point the Australian captain Bill Woodfull, one of the batsmen who was hit, said: 'There are two teams out there, only one of them is playing cricket.' The England tour manager, Pelham Warner, who had been one of Jardine's champions as captain, urged him to curb the Bodyline tactics but the stubborn skipper just dismissed Warner's requests. While Larwood, the great exponent of Bodyline, was excommunicated by English cricket, Jardine continued to captain England in two more series. He always defended his tactics, though the laws of the game were subsequently changed to outlaw the positioning of more than two fielders behind square on the leg side.

JAVED MIANDAD

(Pakistan)

Pakistan's emergence as an international force in the 1970s and 1980s was founded on two fundamentals – Imran Khan and Javed Miandad. They were two contrasting characters. Miandad was a fearless, feisty battler from Karachi while Imran was the educated, westernised superstar from Lahore. In 1981 at Perth Miandad clashed with Australian fast bowler Dennis Lillee, who then kicked Miandad. The Pakistani raised his bat as if to hit Lillee in what *Wisden* described as a 'wretched affair'. Lillee was fined by Australia who sought an apology from Miandad, which was not forthcoming.

Miandad was discovered by Abdul Hafeez Kardar, Pakistan's first Test captain, who described the young batsman as 'the find of the decade'. Miandad certainly lived up to the billing. It was only in late 2015 that he was overtaken by Younis Khan as Pakistan's leading all-time Test run-scorer: his total of 8,832 runs having stood since his last Test in 1993. He made 163 on his Test debut against New Zealand in 1976 and scored his first double century four innings later. He benefited from not being given out lbw in a home Test until 1985 (in the days when umpires came from the host nation) but he was still effective away from home too, averaging forty-five with the bat (as opposed to sixty-one at home).

He reserved some of his best batting for India, against whom Miandad made his highest Test score of 280 not out in 1983. But he will be forever remembered for his match-winning last-ball six to beat India in the final of a one-day tournament in Sharjah in 1986. He finished with 116 not out as Pakistan won with only one wicket standing. Miandad is one of only two players – the other being Sachin Tendulkar – to have played in five World

Cup tournaments. He made half-centuries in the semi-final and final of the 1992 tournament, which Pakistan won. He has also had three separate stints as coach of Pakistan.

55   P

Iz

Inzamam-
ul-Haq

INZAMAM-UL-HAQ

(Pakistan)

'Inzy' was one of Pakistan's greatest batsmen, for sure, and had an impressively lengthy tenure as captain of one of the more turbulent cricketing nations. He is one of only ten men to have scored more than 20,000 runs across the three international formats, he is Pakistan's third highest all-time Test run-scorer and his stunning innings of 329 against New Zealand in 2002 is Pakistan's highest individual Test score.

Yet two uniquely bizarre incidents, a decade apart, effectively bookend the career of this mild-mannered man. In 1996, Pakistan were playing a one-day international against India in Toronto. These were the gold-rush days for international cricket – play whenever and wherever to make a quick buck. The Asian diaspora in North America was, and still is, a lucrative and captive market. Inzamam, who was an advertisement for the larger gentleman, was goaded by an Indian fan who called him, among other things, *aloo* (potato). Inzamam waded into the crowd with a bat threatening to attack his abuser. 'If not for the spectators and security staff curbing him, he would have broken the head of that guy,' an eyewitness said. Inzamam was banned for two ODIs, a punishment that in hindsight seems lenient.

In 2006, Pakistan were at The Oval in the final Test of a four-match series against England, in which they were already 2-0 down. Without a great deal of fanfare, the Australian umpire Darrell Hair penalised Pakistan five runs for allegedly (and illegally) changing the condition of the ball. Ball-tampering is one of cricket's murky taboos, often suspected but rarely proven. To be publicly accused of cheating is a big deal and Inzamam, as captain, was ultimately responsible. He looked bemused and shocked but not apparently angry and there was no sign of the furore to follow when the players left the field for the tea interval. After the traditional twenty-minute break, the umpires appeared, as did England's batsmen but no Pakistan players. The best part of an hour later, with still no resumption, it was decreed that Pakistan had forfeited the Test – the first such occurrence in more than 1,800 matches and 129 years. The controversy raged in the media for days.

BRIAN CLOSE

(England)

In 1949 Brian Close became England's youngest Test cricketer at 18 years, 149 days. In 1976, after a nine-year absence from the team, he was recalled at the age of forty-five, to face down West Indies' pace attack that was causing England so much difficulty. In one memorable over from Michael Holding at Manchester, the balding left-hander, batting bare-headed in the pre-helmet era, took several blows on his body and barely flinched. Bravery, almost to an absurd degree, was one of Close's attributes. His autobiography was titled *I Don't Bruise Easily* and he once said: 'How can the ball hurt you? It's only on you for a second.' Another example of his eccentricity was to discuss the prospect of boxing for a heavyweight world title: 'I might get knocked out, but no one could hurt me. I could beat Ali and Frazier on the same night.'

As a player, Close didn't fulfil his potential but he was a successful, influential captain for Yorkshire and briefly for England. He skippered his county to four County Championship titles in the 1960s, a period of success that would not be replicated for a generation. He also led England to five Test wins in 1967 but was cut adrift after the authorities took exception to accusations of time-wasting in a match for Yorkshire. Later in his career, he moved to Somerset where he was responsible for mentoring their young, tearaway all-rounder, Ian Botham.

TONY GREIG

(England)

A man of contradictions, Tony Greig was a huge, and hugely talented all-round cricketer: he captained England having emigrated from South Africa, provided West Indies with their easiest ever team-talk after an ill-advised comment and later was the key recruiter of players for Kerry Packer's breakaway World Series Cricket in 1977. 'Here is the Nordic superman in the flesh, but although he has the fiercely competitive quality on the field, Greig is a friendly gentle soul off it,' wrote Basil Easterbrook, in *Wisden*, of the man who was 1.98 m and blond.

As a batsman, Greig was always up for a battle. Five of his eight Test centuries came overseas, including one as captain in India in 1976–77 when he had a temperature, and which Greig considered his finest innings. It was the only century on either side in the second Test at Kolkata and it helped England to a ten-wicket win and a series triumph in India for the first time since the 1930s. His bowling, meanwhile was multi-faceted: he was essentially a brisk medium-pace swing bowler who could extract steep bounce because of his height. But in the Caribbean, for example, he was able to switch to bowling sharpish off-spinners.

Greig was adept at creating storms of controversy. In a Test in the Caribbean in 1974, he ran out the West Indies' Alvin Kallicharran as the batsman left his crease at the end of a day's play. Greig was forced to withdraw the appeal and Kallicharran was reinstated. In 1976, before a Test series against West Indies, Greig said that he was 'not really quite sure they're [West Indies] as good as everyone thinks they are'. Then he added infamously: 'If they get on top they're magnificent cricketers but, if they're down, they grovel, and I intend … to make them grovel.' The context of a white man from South Africa in the mid seventies making these comments understandably flicked a switch in the West Indies players. Batsman Gordon Greenidge said the comments 'triggered off a feeling of contempt around the team': they destroyed England with an era-defining display of glorious batting and domineering, aggressive pace bowling.

Greig's involvement with World Series Cricket was viewed by most cricket fans in England as an act of betrayal. He emigrated to Australia and became a fixture in the Channel 9 commentary box until his untimely death aged sixty-six in 2012.

58   E

Pt

Pietersen

KEVIN PIETERSEN

(England)

An off-spin bowler and lower-order batsman in Natal, Kevin Pietersen left his native South Africa for England (he has an English mother) and reinvented himself as one of the most explosive, prolific and idiosyncratic batsmen of modern times. Tall, athletic and ambitious, Pietersen honed a unique batting style and developed strokes all of his own. There was the 'flamingo' – a whipped on-drive through mid-wicket finishing with one leg in the air – and the switch-hit, where the hands were swapped on the bat handle as the bowler reached the crease. When he switch-hit the Sri Lankan Muttiah Muralitharan for six in a 2006 Test match at Birmingham, the cricket world stopped, open-mouthed and asked to see a TV replay.

A showman on and off the field, Pietersen emerged as one of England's Ashes heroes in the epic series of 2005. Sporting a blond streak through his dark brown hair, Pietersen took on Australia's bowlers in the final Test at The Oval, scoring 158 daring and breathtaking runs in the drawn match that secured England's first triumph over Australia for a generation. He scored more than 8,000 runs in 104 Tests for England, and plenty more in the limited-overs formats. He was man of the tournament in England's 2010 triumph at the World Twenty20, their first global title.

In 2012 he was briefly suspended by England for sending insulting text messages about the captain Andrew Strauss to members of the South African team. Then in 2014, following a 5-0 Ashes defeat in Australia, he was cut adrift completely from the England team, a saga that rumbled on for more than a year.

Column 9

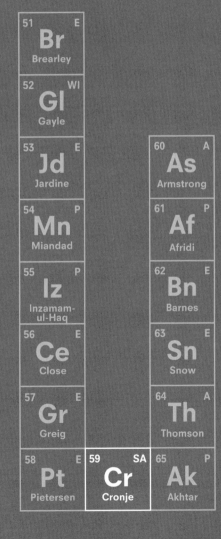

51	E
Br	
Brearley	

52	WI
Gl	
Gayle	

53	E
Jd	
Jardine	

54	P
Mn	
Miandad	

55	P
Iz	
Inzamam-ul-Haq	

56	E
Ce	
Close	

57	E
Gr	
Greig	

58	E
Pt	
Pietersen	

60	A
As	
Armstrong	

61	P
Af	
Afridi	

62	E
Bn	
Barnes	

63	E
Sn	
Snow	

64	A
Th	
Thomson	

59	SA
Cr	
Cronje	

65	P
Ak	
Akhtar	

HANSIE CRONJE

(South Africa)

The former South African captain is not so much a maverick as a villain. Cricket's self-delusion that the game was clean and corruption-free was blown apart in April 2000. After initially denying the allegations of New Delhi police who had recordings of a phone conversation between Hansie Cronje and an Indian bookmaker, Sanjay Chawla, Cronje confessed in a 3 a.m. phone call to his boss Ali Bacher, the head of the South African cricket board, that he had not been entirely honest.

What emerged was a grubby, shameful tale of greed and corruption. Cronje had received hundreds of thousands of dollars from illegal bookmakers in return for team and match information, or for manipulating passages of play in matches. He denied ever fixing the result of a match. He did also try to coerce his more vulnerable teammates to get involved. In January 2000 during a Test at Centurion against England that had been badly rain-affected, he had suggested to his opposite number, Nasser Hussain, that they should contrive a positive finish to the match, rather than simply let it peter out as a draw. At the time this was considered an imaginative and progressive gesture by Cronje. But it emerged months later that in fact he had received 53,000 rand (around £5,000) and a leather jacket from a bookmaker. Cronje was banned for life from all cricketing activities.

Before the match-fixing scandal, the fiercely determined and God-fearing Cronje had been a successful captain of his country, moulding South Africa into a credible force in Test and one-day cricket after their post-apartheid readmission. He was ultra-competitive, once thrusting a stump through the umpires' room door after a Test at Adelaide out of his frustration at a decision that went against his side. He was an attacking middle-order right-handed batsman especially effective in one-day cricket.

But it is the match-fixing scandal for which he is remembered. To add to the intrigue of the whole affair, Cronje was killed in a plane crash in South Africa two years after his admissions. Match-fixing, real or imagined, continues to dog cricket, famously in 2010 when three Pakistan players were banned following a newspaper sting involving the bowling of no-balls to order in a Test match at Lord's.

Column 10

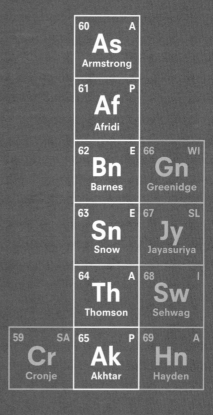

60 A **As** Armstrong	
61 P **Af** Afridi	
62 E **Bn** Barnes	**66** WI **Gn** Greenidge
63 E **Sn** Snow	**67** SL **Jy** Jayasuriya
64 A **Th** Thomson	**68** I **Sw** Sehwag
59 SA **Cr** Cronje	**65** P **Ak** Akhtar	**69** A **Hn** Hayden

WARWICK ARMSTRONG

(Australia)

Warwick Armstrong captained Australia to eight successive Test victories over England at the start of the 1920s including, in 1920–21, the only 5-0 Ashes whitewash until Australia achieved the feat twice in 2006–07 and 2013–14. At the start of his career he was a relatively slim man but by the time he came to England in 1921 he weighed 139 kg (22 st) and was known as 'The Big Ship'. He was a divisive figure, not renowned for happily accepting the umpire's decision. The England batting legend Jack Hobbs once described an incident in which he referred to Armstrong as 'nasty and unsportsmanlike'. He refused to tour England in 1912 because of a dispute with the Australian authorities about how the team was selected. His career was punctuated by other disagreements, often about money.

Once when fielding on the boundary, a newspaper blew from the crowd on to the pitch; Armstrong picked it up and started reading. He was an inelegant, but effective, batsman and scored six centuries in his fifty Tests. In his first Test in 1902, he batted at number eleven and, with Reggie Duff, helped put on Test cricket's first century partnership for the tenth wicket. He also played Australian Rules football for South Melbourne.

SHAHID AFRIDI

(Pakistan)

In the unhinged world of Pakistan cricket, it takes something to be known as an alternative character. Shahid 'Boom Boom' Afridi's talents are considerable – from skilful varietals of leg-spin through to heavy, almost deranged, hitting. Tall and strapping, with a certain bounce in his step, he has never been a consistent performer but that is part of the charm and the mystery.

Afridi made his debut for Pakistan in 1996 aged sixteen and in only his second one-day international (but his first innings) he smashed the world champions, Sri Lanka, for a thirty-seven-ball century, an ODI record. He has two of the fastest one-day centuries ever scored and a couple of seventy-eight-ball Test hundreds too. In 2010 he captained Pakistan against Australia in a Test on neutral soil at Lord's. With his side struggling on eighty-three for five, he hit thirty-one off fifteen balls, with four fours and two sixes, in a cameo that was bizarre even by his standards. It had been his first Test for four years and it turned out to be his last as he resigned the captaincy after the match, which Pakistan lost.

A year earlier on the same ground Afridi had enjoyed a career highlight when his unbeaten fifty-four led Pakistan to victory over Sri Lanka in the final of the World Twenty20 tournament. He has rarely been far from controversy and has incurred bans for scouring the pitch with his studs and also for ball-tampering when he appeared to try to bite the ball as if it were an apple.

SYDNEY BARNES

(England)

Test cricket is the pinnacle, so goes the standard mantra of the on-message modern player, most often in reference to the proliferation of the limited-overs game. Not to S. F. Barnes it wasn't, even though a case can be made that he is England's greatest ever bowler. He is hard to categorise: he bowled brisk medium-pace and was a pioneer in using the seam to move the ball off the pitch. He described himself as a spinner.

Between 1901 and 1914, Barnes took 189 wickets in twenty-seven Tests at the absurdly skinny average of sixteen runs apiece. Of those wickets, seventy-seven were taken on the traditionally batsman-friendly pitches of Australia. No one in history can better his forty-nine wickets in a series in South Africa in 1913–14. He played only four of the five Tests, missing one because the authorities wouldn't pay for his wife's accommodation. He was an aloof and difficult character, from whom 'a chill wind of antagonism blew on the sunniest day', according to Neville Cardus. Barnes was a professional driven by money and preferred to play club cricket and minor counties cricket for Staffordshire rather than first-class cricket for Warwickshire and Lancashire. He was still playing for Staffordshire into his fifties.

JOHN SNOW

(England)

The son of a vicar and a published poet, John Snow was certainly not your average cricketer. Or, indeed, your average anything. A magnificently hostile fast bowler, he played only forty-nine Tests, taking 202 wickets, despite being for much of the 1960s and 1970s comfortably England's best 'quick'.

In 1971, Snow covered more ground than many manage in a career. At the start of the year, he was integral to England's Ashes victory in Australia, during which he bowled with venom. In the final decisive Test at Sydney, there were protests when he hit the Australian tail-ender Terry Jenner in the face and was warned for intimidatory bowling. Later in the same innings, he broke a hand on the boundary fence trying to take a catch. Back in England, he was twice disciplined by his county Sussex for 'not trying' and disciplined for barging the Indian opening batsman Sunil Gavaskar. It was also the year that his first book of poetry was published.

64	A
Th	
Thomson	

JEFF THOMSON

(Australia)

One of the fastest bowlers ever to play the game, 'Thommo' was very much his own man, both in terms of his extraordinary bowling style and also his carefree attitude to life. 'Aw, mate, I just shuffle up and go wang,' was how Jeff Thomson described his bowling action that ran contrary to most of the orthodoxies of fast bowling. He didn't have a long run-up: instead, all his speed was generated by a body action that was part catapult and part javelin thrower. Rather than the bowling hand being next to his face as he prepared to deliver the ball, it appeared from behind his back. 'Thomson's tremendous strength – or perhaps some feature of his perfectly fair but "hurling" action – enabled him to get the ball up from a fuller length that any fast bowler I had seen,' wrote John Thicknesse in *Wisden*.

It was not a bowling action pre-disposed towards longevity and Thomson played a relatively modest fifty-one Tests over a twelve-year period from his debut in 1972. He took 128 of his 200 Test wickets in a three-and-a-half year period from late 1974 until early 1978. He was at his devastating and terrifying best in the 1974–75 Ashes, a series before which he had said: 'I enjoy hitting a batsman more than getting him out. I like to see blood on the pitch.' He did both, taking thirty–three wickets at 17.93 each before injuring himself playing tennis on a rest day during the penultimate Test. He also caused physical harm to a number of England batsmen, including David Lloyd, now a popular TV commentator, who was hit in the groin so hard that his abdominal protector was turned inside out.

SHOAIB AKHTAR

(Pakistan)

'The list of misdemeanours is impossibly long,' wrote the Pakistani journalist and author, Osman Samiuddin, on ESPNcricinfo. Shoaib Akhtar, or the 'Rawalpindi Express' to use his tabloid moniker, is the bowler of the fastest officially recorded delivery but his career was blighted by a range of issues including doping offences, legal battles with the Pakistan board, fights with teammates and allegations of ball-tampering. 'He was incredibly fast, swung the new ball and old ball, and his overs and spells were an event to watch,' wrote Kevin Pietersen, in the *Daily Telegraph*, having selected Shoaib in a best Test XI of cricketers he played with and against.

Shoaib bowled the first 100 mph (161 kph) ball at the World Cup in 2003 in South Africa though the delivery itself, to England's Nick Knight, was far from unplayable. One that was unplayable, though, was a ball that writer and former England bowler, Mike Selvey, claims is the fastest he's ever seen. It was a yorker (a ball speared in at the batsman's feet) from around the wicket, and therefore a wide angle, at the left-handed New Zealand captain, Stephen Fleming, in the semi-final of the 1999 World Cup. It was 'only' ninety-two mph (148 kph) and, according to ESPNcricinfo, 'Fleming jammed his bat down on it about an hour too late'. Tony Greig, commentating for television, described the delivery as 'absolutely unreal'.

Aggressors
& Enforcers

'To bowl quick is to revel in the glad animal action; to thrill in the physical prowess and to enjoy a certain sneaking feeling of superiority over the other mortals who play the game.' These are the words of the erudite Frank Tyson, the England fast bowler of the 1950s, from his autobiography *A Typhoon Called Tyson*. But that glad animal action of physical domination and superiority is not exclusive to the pace bowlers, though they make up a hefty chunk of this chapter.

Those batsmen who go hard at the bowlers are the box-office boys, the game-changers. Increasingly, aggressive batting is the norm, aided by ever more powerful bats. Where once scoring at three runs an over would be considered a good lick, now that would be thought of as positively dilatory. Modern batsmen think nothing of hurtling along at a run a ball, or faster in fifty-over matches or Twenty20. Spin bowlers can be aggressive too. As with so much in cricket, it's all in the mind.

Column 11

60 A **As** Armstrong	70 E **Js** Jessop
61 P **Af** Afridi	71 A **B** Bradman
62 E **Bn** Barnes	66 WI **Gn** Greenidge	72 WI **Wk** Weekes
63 E **Sn** Snow	67 SL **Jy** Jayasuriya	73 A **Ci** I. Chappell
64 A **Th** Thomson	68 I **Sw** Sehwag	74 WI **Ld** Lloyd
65 P **Ak** Akhtar	69 A **Hn** Hayden	75 WI **Rv** V. Richards

GORDON GREENIDGE

(West Indies)

A powerful brooding presence at the top of the West Indies' batting order from the mid 1970s through the whole of the 1980s, Gordon Greenidge was an unusual character. Born in Barbados but raised in England, he returned to the Caribbean and was not easily accepted. 'He was a very serious man who ... didn't entirely fit into the West Indies dressing room, which was usually a place of fun and laughter,' said Tony Cozier, the veteran commentator on West Indies cricket. His opening partnership with Desmond Haynes yielded 6,482 runs and sixteen stands of 100 or more, both of which remain all-time Test records. Haynes was hardly a slowcoach himself but relatively speaking he was the rock and Greenidge provided the fire.

It became something of a truism around world cricket that if Greenidge ever started limping, you knew he was on for a century. Injury, perceived or otherwise, seemed to make him play better. 'I like to feel I am going to take the fight to the bowlers,' he said. His square cut was among the most vicious shots any batsman has ever played. He went six years without scoring a Test century (1977–83) but became more prolific as he got older. The first of his four double hundreds, at Lord's in 1984, was an iconic innings. Set what looked like a challenging target of 342 to win in less than a day by England, West Indies won at a gallop by nine wickets with 11.5 overs to spare. Greenidge spanked twenty-nine fours in scoring 214 not out: 'the innings of his life', said *Wisden*.

SANATH JAYASURIYA

(Sri Lanka)

He didn't quite invent the concept of a hard-hitting batsman at the top of the order in one-day matches – that honour falls to Mark Greatbatch and the lateral-thinking

New Zealanders at the 1992 World Cup – but Sri Lanka's explosive left-hander Sanath Jayasuriya certainly set the standard for others to follow.

For the first four years of his one-day international career he was a left-arm spinner who batted, without much success, in the middle order. The switch to opening proved devastating. His first hundred came in his seventy-first match in 1994, against New Zealand. Two years later at the World Cup he properly made his name and set Sri Lanka on the way to their improbable triumph. In a group match against India he and his fellow opener Romesh Kaluwitharana hit forty-two off the first three overs of their run chase. *Wisden* reported: 'Jayasuriya charged on, though his final statistics of seventy-nine in seventy-six balls, with nine fours and two sixes, seemed sedate after his initial rampage.' In the quarter-final he brought England to their knees, smashing eighty off forty-four balls as Sri Lanka won with almost ten overs to spare.

Jayasuriya was equally destructive in the five-day game. In 1997 he scored 340 against India in Colombo and was involved in a partnership of 576 with Roshan Mahanama, then the largest stand for any wicket in Test history (though since overtaken by another Sri Lanka pair, Kumar Sangakkara and Mahela Jayawardene).

VIRENDER SEHWAG

(India)

No batsman (with at least 2,000 runs) scored faster than the eighty-two runs per hundred balls Virender Sehwag managed in his 104 Tests for India through the 2000s. 'The overwhelming impression is that he wants every delivery to yield him a four or a six,' wrote Ravi Shastri, the India all-rounder turned commentator, of this brutal opening batsman. Sehwag did not have a sophisticated technique: indeed he barely had a technique at all. He remained still at the crease and woe betide any bowler who gave him room to free his arms, especially through the off side, because the ball would disappear from his bat as fast as it had arrived.

It is a curious paradox that for all the patient accumulators India have had over the years, no one had scored 250 in a Test innings until 2001. The bar was initially raised by V. V. S. Laxman but between 2004 and 2009, Sehwag helped himself to scores of 254, 293, 309 and 319, the latter being India's highest individual Test score. He is one of only four batsmen to have scored two Test triple centuries. The 309 made against Pakistan at Multan in 2004 was significant because it set up an Indian victory but Sehwag regarded the 319 as a better innings: it was made against a good South African pace attack and came after he had spent two exhausting days in the field at Chennai. It was inevitably the fastest triple hundred ever made, in only 278 balls.

It goes almost without saying that Sehwag was also a plunderer of runs in one-day cricket, too, and in late 2011, in the twilight of his career, he posted the then highest score in a fifty-over match, hitting 219 against West Indies at Indore.

MATTHEW HAYDEN

(Australia)

Tall, brutish and square-jawed, Matthew Hayden was always on the attack with word and deed. It took the left-handed opener from rural Queensland three years in the late 1990s to play his first three Tests for Australia. Considered technically deficient against quick bowling, he then had to wait until 2000 for a prolonged run in the team.

Then for the next seven years he established one of the game's great first-wicket alliances with Justin Langer, which produced more runs than any such partnership apart from Greenidge and Haynes. Langer was short, gritty and tough; Hayden, huge, expansive and equally tough. Hayden started the ignition for the Australian juggernaut in the 1990s and early 2000s. There was no circumspection, as used to be the tradition for opening batsmen, no seeing off the new ball. Instead, opening bowlers got used to the sight of Hayden giving them the charge, smacking the brand new ball straight back past them.

From January 2001 to December 2002, Hayden scored eleven centuries (out of his career total of thirty) in twenty-five Tests, averaging sixty-seven. In late 2003, he broke the world record for the highest Test innings. Given the poor nature of the Zimbabwean opposition, the innings did not get the credit others of its type receive and the record was reclaimed a few months later by Brian Lara.

Column 12

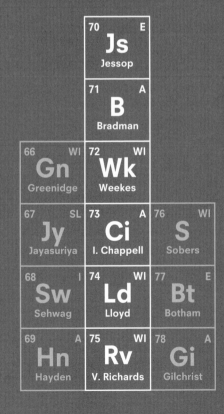

70	E
Js	
Jessop	

71	A
B	
Bradman	

66	WI
Gn	
Greenidge	

72	WI
Wk	
Weekes	

67	SL
Jy	
Jayasuriya	

73	A
Ci	
I. Chappell	

76	WI
S	
Sobers	

68	I
Sw	
Sehwag	

74	WI
Ld	
Lloyd	

77	E
Bt	
Botham	

69	A
Hn	
Hayden	

75	WI
Rv	
V. Richards	

78	A
Gi	
Gilchrist	

70	E
Js	
Jessop	

GILBERT JESSOP

(England)

Gilbert Jessop was one of the greatest hitters of a cricket ball. His match-winning century, made in only seventy-seven minutes at The Oval in 1902, remains one of the iconic innings in Ashes history.

Originally a fast bowler, Jessop injured his back in 1899 and became renowned for his batting, hitting hard from his unusual stance that gave him the nickname of 'The Croucher'. In that innings at The Oval, Jessop hit 104 out of 139 while he was at the crease, including seventeen fours. This was at a time when a six was only awarded if the ball went out of the ground. 'All things considered a more astonishing display has never been seen,' reported *Wisden*. 'What he did would have been scarcely possible under the same circumstances to any other living batsman.'

Jessop played only eighteen Tests but scored heavily and quickly in county cricket for Gloucestershire. His fifty-three first-class centuries were made an average of eighty-two runs per hour. At Brighton in 1903, he hit 286 out of 355 in only three hours, an astonishing rate and proportion of scoring even by contemporary standards. He was also an exceptional fielder in the covers.

DON BRADMAN

(Australia)

Statistical comparisons, of which cricket is so beloved, can often be misleading. But when it comes to deciding the identity of the best batsman ever to hold a bat, the numbers tell you all you need to know. Don Bradman's Test batting average of 99.94 is almost 40 runs per innings better than the next on the list of those who have played at least twenty Test innings.

It is hard to overstate the impact that The Don and his exploits had on the whole country of Australia in the inter-war period during which he was in his pomp. 'His was the contemporary Australian journey,' wrote the esteemed writer and historian Gideon Haigh. Growing up in rural New South Wales, learning to bat by hitting a golf ball with a cricket stump against a cylindrical water tank, Bradman became a global sporting superstar. 'He was simultaneously imprisoned by fame to a degree he could not readily accept,' wrote E. W. Swanton in an article for *Wisden* published after Bradman's death in 2001.

Only 1.70 m tall, Bradman was not physically imposing but he had an ability to dictate terms in almost any situation: he was not so much an aggressor as a dominator with ruthless efficiency. He scored 300 in an innings six times in first-class cricket yet on only twelve occasions in his career did he bat for six hours or more (the standard length of a day's play). As impressive as the volume of runs he scored was the speed at which he scored them. On the list of the most runs scored in a Test-match day, Bradman's name appears twice: the overall record for 309 at Leeds in 1930 and 271, also at Leeds, four years later.

He made his debut for Australia in 1928 against England, was dropped for the next Test but returned for the third and made a century. From then on, he was pretty much unstoppable. In the 1930 Ashes series in England, he scored 974 runs in five matches at an average of 139. Such fear did he strike into English hearts that for the next series in Australia in 1932–33, the England captain Douglas Jardine devised a plan to nullify The Don that involved fast, short-pitched bowling. It became known in the Australian press as 'Bodyline' and that series, which England won 4-1, is the most famous, or infamous, in all cricket. Bradman still averaged fifty-six, though.

In the 1936–37 Ashes, Australia were 2-0 down but won the last three Tests to win the series with Bradman scoring 13, 270, 26 and 212 in those victories. In his final Test innings at The Oval in 1948, he required only four runs to finish with a career average of exactly 100. Yet, having received three cheers from the England team as he walked to the crease, he was bowled by a googly from leg-spinner Eric Hollies for a second-ball duck.

EVERTON WEEKES

(West Indies)

'He set out to hammer bowlers,' said Richie Benaud, the former Australia captain, of Everton Weekes. Along with Frank Worrell and Clyde Walcott, Weekes formed the 'Three Ws', all Barbadians who were the bedrock of the West Indian middle-order batting during the 1950s. He played a significant part in establishing West Indies as a potent global cricketing force. In only his fourth Test, in 1948, Weekes began a run of five Test centuries in successive innings: a record that has never been surpassed. Yet it could even have been bettered had he not been run out on ninety against India at Chennai. 'The secret of his success was quickness of eye, foot and wrist,' reported *Wisden*, which also remarked that this series, the first between West Indies and India, marked a changing of the guard with George Headley not missed.

On the famous 1950 tour of England – West Indies' first Test series victory in England – Weekes was consistent again, averaging 56 and teaming up spectacularly with Worrell in a stand of 283 for the fourth wicket in the third Test at Nottingham. His career Test average of fifty-eight is one of the highest of all time.

IAN CHAPPELL

(Australia)

Sleeves rolled up, shirt unbuttoned to his mid-riff, the moustachioed Ian Chappell was not a man to back down, whether it was taking on fast bowlers with the hook shot, leading from the front or in regular conflict with administrators.

Chappell's particular brand of aggression was hugely successful. He picked up the Australian team after they had surprisingly lost the Ashes at home in 1970–71 and did not lose any of the subsequent seven series he captained. Despite leading the team he was always an anti-establishment figure, bitterly resenting the master–servant relationship that existed between administrators and players at that time. He unashamedly jumped ship to Kerry Packer's World Series Cricket in the mid 1970s, along with many of his high-profile teammates. The lot of the professional cricketer changed – for the better – from that moment.

In the final Ashes Test of 1972 at The Oval, Chappell scored a century in a double-century stand with his brother Greg to help Australia level the series against England. It wasn't enough to regain the Ashes but it was a turning point for Australia. The Chappell brothers – chalk and cheese as personalities – were prolific partners at the crease. Against New Zealand at Wellington in 1974, the brothers both, remarkably, scored a century in each innings of the Test. The Ashes of 1974–75 was Ian's most memorable triumph as England were blown away by the relentless pace of Dennis Lillee and Jeff Thomson. A pace battery was central to the Ashes being retained in 1975 in England, with Chappell scoring 192 (an innings 'which was always aggressive in intent', according to *Wisden*) at The Oval in his final match as captain. In retirement, he became a highly respected TV commentator with strong opinions and sound judgement.

CLIVE LLOYD

(West Indies)

Beneath the flower-pot hat, behind the spectacles and drooping moustache was a man of gentle countenance. Yet with a bat in his hand or with his fast bowlers at his command, Clive Lloyd could change a game in a single session of play. He was the architect of modern West Indies cricket: a father figure but also a ruthlessly successful tactician and strategist. Standing 1.95 m with a slightly stooping gait, Lloyd wielded a heavier bat than most. But his left-handed batting, while destructive, also possessed a languid grace. Mike Selvey, the former England bowler, described how one particular shot from Lloyd for Lancashire against his West Indian teammate Wayne Daniel 'connected prodigiously from a spot on the blade so sweet it was a danger to diabetics'. One of the most famous quotes from the BBC radio commentator John Arlott described one shot by Lloyd as 'the stroke of a man knocking a thistle top off with a walking stick'.

Lloyd took over the West Indies captaincy in 1974 and, after a chastening 5-1 Test series defeat in Australia in 1975–76, steeled himself and his team. Founded on serious physical fitness, athletic fielding, a ferocious four-pronged pace attack and aggressive batting, his side lost only two out of eighteen Test series under Lloyd's command and were unbeaten in the last nine of his tenure until 1985, when Viv Richards took over. Lloyd also led them to victory in the first two World Cup tournaments in 1975 and 1979. In the 1975 final against Australia at Lord's, he scored an eighty-five-ball century and was man of the match.

VIV RICHARDS

(West Indies)

A Viv Richards innings began as soon as he emerged from the dressing room on to the field of play: with his maroon West Indies cap (never a helmet) at an angle, gum chewed rhythmically, the broad shoulders would be loosened with a swirl of the bat while the hips rolled in a swagger to the crease that was uniquely Viv. After a few taps of the pitch with his bat and then a few taps of the top of the bat handle into the palm of his hand, he was ready to go. He wanted everyone to know that this was his stage and few batsmen in history have presented themselves to the bowler and fielders with such simmering intent. He had such belief in his own ability that although his batting was beautiful – as well as brutal – it was also highly unorthodox. His first movement was often across his stumps and bowlers would think they could have him lbw only to see a decent delivery disappear through the leg side to the boundary.

Along with the fast bowler Andy Roberts, Viv Richards was the first Antiguan to play for West Indies in 1974 and he announced himself immediately, making 192 not out in his second Test. In 1976 he scored 1,710 Test runs at an average of 90, a record for a calendar year that stood until 2006. In England that year he made 829 runs in four Tests, including two double centuries. In the final Test of a 3-0 series win, he scored 291, which would remain his highest Test score. The innings contained thirty-eight fours and was an exhibition of glorious destruction.

In a 1984 one-day international against England at Manchester, Richards rescued his side with 189 not out, then the highest ODI score. With West Indies 166 for 9, he batted with outrageous audacity to lift them to what became a comfortable winning total: one of his five sixes disappeared out of the Old Trafford ground.

A year later, Richards took over the West Indies captaincy from Clive Lloyd and continued the side's amazing success. Without the guile or diplomacy skills of Lloyd, he was often a contentious, confrontational figure as captain. In 1986 against England, on his home ground of Antigua, he hit the fastest Test century of all time, taking only fifty-six balls, with sometimes as many as nine men on the boundary. He was also, certainly early in his career, a brilliantly athletic fielder and his two run-outs in the first World Cup final in 1975 changed the game. He scored a match-winning century in the final of the next tournament in 1979.

Column 13

	79 A **Or** O'Reilly
70 E **Js** Jessop	**80** A **W** Warne
71 A **B** Bradman	**81** A **Sp** Spofforth
72 WI **Wk** Weekes	**82** E **Lw** Larwood
73 A **Ci** I. Chappell	**76** WI **S** Sobers	**83** A **Ln** Lindwall
74 WI **Ld** Lloyd	**77** E **Bt** Botham	**84** E **Tm** Trueman
75 WI **Rv** V. Richards	**78** A **Gi** Gilchrist	**85** E **Ty** Tyson

76	WI
S	
Sobers	

GARRY SOBERS

(West Indies)

Just as there is no equivocation that Don Bradman is the best batsman in history, so there is no questioning the status of Sir Garfield St Aubrun Sobers as quite simply the greatest all-round cricketer the game has seen. As a left-arm bowler, he could operate at whatever pace he chose and impart swing or spin. And he swung a bat, also left-handed, with the sort of uninhibited, flowing arc seen when Roger Federer has a racket in his hand.

Born in Barbados, Sobers played for his island at sixteen and for West Indies at seventeen. His maiden Test century against Pakistan at Kingston in 1958, aged twenty-one, was his highest – indeed anyone's highest. By scoring 365 not out, he broke Len Hutton's twenty-year-old individual Test batting record. The record stood until 1994 when it was broken by Brian Lara. Sobers would make another twenty-five centuries, including three big ones in the 1966 series victory in England – in which he made 722 runs at an average of 103 and took twenty wickets.

In 1968, playing for Nottinghamshire against Glamorgan at Swansea, Sobers produced one of the game's most iconic feats, becoming the first man to hit all six balls of an over for six. Sobers was trying to set up a declaration while the hapless bowler Malcolm Nash, a left-arm seamer, was experimenting with slow bowling – an experiment that he did not repeat.

Perhaps his greatest innings came at Melbourne in 1971. By now thirty-five, Sobers was playing for a Rest of the World XI against Australia because the proposed tour by South Africa had been cancelled following the country's sporting isolation. Facing Australia's young tearaway Dennis Lillee, Sobers had fuelled their tussle by bowling bouncers at Lillee, who told his teammates he would respond in kind. Sobers made 254. 'An incredible innings,' said the Australian captain Ian Chappell while Don Bradman said it was the best innings he had ever seen in Australia.

IAN BOTHAM

(England)

England's greatest all-round player, and still probably the country's most famous cricket personality, Ian Botham was a bullocking force of nature who swept through the game in the 1970s and 1980s. Self-belief and bravado underpinned his dramatic career that gleamed for three brilliant years at the end of the seventies and then exploded intermittently after that in a series of improbable achievements.

Botham took five wickets on his Test debut in 1977 against Australia and never looked – or stepped – back. A supreme swing bowler, capable of moving the ball both ways, and an orthodox but ultra-aggressive batsman, Botham launched his career at breakneck speed. He reached 100 wickets in the then shortest time on record of only two years and five days, and in 1980 became only the second man to score a century and take ten wickets in the same match. Soon after that phenomenal match against India at Mumbai, Botham became England captain, aged only twenty-four. It was a brief and unsuccessful reign and diluted his superhuman powers.

As if to confirm the point, no sooner had he resigned the captaincy – after two matches of the 1981 Ashes series – than his mojo returned. He produced three of the most memorable performances in post-war English cricket history in consecutive Tests to turn the series on its head: a counter-attacking 149 not out at Leeds that set up a victory after England were staring at defeat; a bowling spell of five wickets for a single run in twenty-eight balls to scupper Australia's pursuit of another small total in the next Test; then a majestic innings of 118 in the fifth Test to set up a series-clinching victory.

Even as his physical powers diminished later in his career, Botham was able to summon the muse when Australia were the opponents. He took thirty-one wickets in the 1985 home Ashes victory. Then in the return series eighteen months later scored his first Test century for almost three years, as well as taking a series-winning five-wicket haul at Melbourne despite bowling no faster than medium pace because of injury.

ADAM GILCHRIST

(Australia)

Adam Gilchrist was a champion without fuss. 'Incredible talent unsurpassed in the game's history, in a style never before seen,' wrote Ian Healy, his predecessor as Australia wicket-keeper, in *Wisden*.

Gilchrist was a batsman first and wicket-keeper second, essentially creating the template that every other international team tried to follow. That is not to say his keeping wasn't excellent – he formed a rock-solid partnership with Shane Warne – but it was his clean, left-handed ball-striking that set him apart, whether that was opening the batting in one-day internationals or counter-attacking ferociously at number seven in Australia's all-conquering Test side. He wasn't aesthetically pleasing but nor was he ugly – he just smashed it!

Gilchrist had already played seventy-six ODIs before making his Test debut in 1999 against Pakistan and in his second match at Hobart he set the jaw-dropping standard that he would maintain for most of his career. He came in to bat with Australia 126 for five chasing 369, seemingly a lost cause. Gilchrist hit 149 not out off 163 balls, put on 238 with number three Justin Langer, and led them to victory with the loss of only more wicket. For opponents, getting through the Australian top and middle order was not even half the job done. If 'Gilly' found his range, then bad positions were turned around and good positions became impregnable.

At Perth in Australia's 2006–07 Ashes whitewash of England, Gilchrist's powers appeared to be waning yet, on a stiflingly hot Saturday afternoon, he came within a single ball of equalling Viv Richards's record for the fastest Test century. An adopted West Australian, he flogged the England bowlers mercilessly in front of a raucously partisan crowd. Two days later Australia reclaimed the Ashes. A few months later in Barbados, he played the highest, and greatest, innings at a World Cup final. His 149 from 104 balls took Australia to a hat-trick of titles and Gilchrist had been central to all three.

Column 14

		86 WI **Hl** Hall
		87 A **Li** Lillee
	79 A **Or** O'Reilly	**88** WI **Ro** Roberts
	80 A **W** Warne	**89** WI **Ho** Holding
	81 A **Sp** Spofforth	**90** WI **Mh** Marshall
	82 E **Lw** Larwood	**91** WI **Ab** Ambrose
76 WI **S** Sobers	**83** A **Ln** Lindwall	**92** P **Wa** Akram
77 E **Bt** Botham	**84** E **Tm** Trueman	**93** SA **Dn** Donald
78 A **Gi** Gilchrist	**85** E **Ty** Tyson	**94** SA **St** Steyn

BILL O'REILLY

(Australia)

Described by Don Bradman as the greatest bowler he had ever faced or seen, Bill 'Tiger' O'Reilly was a leg-spinner who played 'with the fierce zeal of a fire-and-brimstone missionary', according to Christopher Martin-Jenkins in *The Complete Who's Who of Test Cricketers*. He was 1.88 m tall with a furiously busy bowling action, which was all arms and legs. He bowled with pace and aggression, more in keeping with a fast bowler than a spinner. In that respect he was the begetter of Shane Warne.

O'Reilly took 144 Test wickets at a very tidy average of twenty-two through the 1930s, which was a batsman's era. His twenty-seven wickets in the Bodyline series of 1932–33 were overshadowed by everything else that was going on. In England in 1934 he took twenty-eight wickets, including seven in an innings twice. At Leeds in 1938 he took ten wickets in the match to facilitate a victory that meant Australia retained the Ashes. He dismissed the great Wally Hammond twice in the match and ten times in his career: no bowler got Hammond more often. In fifteen of his twenty-seven Tests O'Reilly teamed up with Clarrie Grimmett, a New Zealand-born leg-spinner who relied on the more traditional virtues of flight and an unerring length. 'With "Grum" at the other end, prepared to pick me up and dust me down, I feared no batsman,' wrote O'Reilly of his old partner. 'Our association must have been one of cricket's greatest success stories of the twentieth century.' O'Reilly played his last Test in 1946 but continued his involvement in the game as an acerbic, witty journalist.

SHANE WARNE

(Australia)

Shane Warne was a leg-spinner in fast bowler's clothing, a unique talent who reinvented a mysterious and fading art. He attacked batsmen in the way pace bowlers did: not in the physical sense but by imposing himself on his opponents, never letting them settle, getting inside their head. But more importantly he was a showman, who demanded attention. 'He was a film star on the set of a cricket field, and he did stuff that, literally, people couldn't believe,' wrote Mark Nicholas, the English broadcaster and colleague of Warne's at Channel 9 in Australia.

Cricket was not even Warne's chosen sport – he originally had ambitions to be an Australian Rules footballer. In 1993 he arrived in England with a burgeoning, but unproven, reputation. His first ball in Ashes cricket, at Manchester, was immediately dubbed 'the ball of the century' and, despite the hyperbole, not without justification. Warne span the ball so hard that he created a drift that took the ball way outside England batsman Mike Gatting's leg stump. Gatting simply stuck his pad at the ball, to defend it, only to see it fizz past his defences and clip the top of his off stump. The look of astonishment on Gatting's face told the story.

Warne took another 707 Test wickets over the next fourteen years, so many of them as memorable as the first and so many crucial to Australia winning yet another Test, yet another series, often from improbable positions. Only in India, where batsmen are so adept at playing spin, was he really blunted. He had a range of subtle skills but he was also a master at pre-match hype, suggesting he had invented a new type of delivery and letting a star-struck media lap it up while secretly knowing the truth might be somewhat different. His ability to shape a script to his own ends was never better exemplified than his 700th Test wicket, which was taken in his penultimate Test on Boxing Day 2006, on his home turf of the Melbourne Cricket Ground in front of almost 90,000 people in the Ashes.

Warne always ploughed his own furrow, preferring not to embrace modern training methods and surviving mostly on cigarettes, chips and pizza. His sexual indiscretions and celebrity liaisons have been as widely reported as his wicket-taking feats.

FRED SPOFFORTH

(Australia)

At 1.91 m, with a handlebar moustache and a curious stooping approach to the crease, Fred 'The Demon' Spofforth certainly lived up to his nickname. According to the historian David Frith in his book *The Fast Men*, Spofforth had the look of Dennis Lillee but the mood of John Snow. He was the first great fast bowler of the international game and the man who proved to the Poms that the Aussies were a force to be reckoned with.

Spofforth had refused to play in the inaugural Test at Melbourne in 1877 because he disagreed with the choice of Australian wicket-keeper, though he played in the second. The following year the Australians toured England for the first time and, at Lord's, Spofforth blew away MCC, W. G. Grace and all. The match lasted a single day with Spofforth taking eleven wickets – six for four in the first innings and five for sixteen in the second as MCC and Ground were dismissed for thirty-three and nineteen respectively. In addition, he 'painfully hurt and prostrated Hornby, compelling him to retire', according to the 1879 *Wisden*, which added that the game was 'one of the most remarkable matches ever played at Lord's'.

Four years later, Spofforth took fourteen wickets in Australia's victory at The Oval – the result that spawned the Ashes. England were sixty-six for four, needing only eighty-five to win in a low-scoring match, when The Demon took control. Four wickets fell, all to him, for nine runs and England ended up losing by seven runs. The mock obituary for the death of English cricket followed in the *Sporting Times* and one of sport's greatest and most enduring rivalries was properly born.

HAROLD LARWOOD

(England)

A Nottinghamshire miner who rose to prominence
swiftly in the 1920s and infamy in the 1930s, Harold
Larwood emigrated to Australia in 1950 to live out the
rest of his days essentially in secluded exile. Having
been the man who fired the bullets of England captain
Douglas Jardine in the Bodyline series of 1932–33,
there was a glorious irony that he should settle –
and be readily accepted – in the land of the men he
vanquished in that most controversial and ill-tempered
Ashes contest.

For a fast bowler, Larwood was not a tall man, only
1.72 m, and he was slight too. But he was strong, a
legacy of his time down the pits. Fuelled by beer and
cigarettes, Larwood made his debut for England in 1926
and impressed on the 1928–29 tour of Australia when
he first encountered Don Bradman, the man his pace
was designed to thwart four years later. In the Bodyline
series, Larwood bowled himself into the ground at the
behest of Jardine. He tore in at the Australians until
blood seeped through the leather of his bowling boots.
When, in the third Test at Adelaide, Larwood hit Australian
captain Bill Woodfull over the heart – the single moment
that defines Bodyline more than any other – Jardine
bellowed: 'Well bowled, Harold.'

Larwood took thirty-three wickets at nineteen runs
apiece in England's 4-1 Bodyline triumph and never
played for England again.

MCC, who ran English cricket then, tried to force
him to write a letter of apology for his part in Bodyline,
which had caused such uproar and placed such strain
on relations between England and Australia. Larwood
refused, saying he had nothing to apologise for. Visitors
to his home in Sydney were always made aware of a
silver ashtray, engraved with the citation: 'To Harold for
the Ashes – 1932–33. From a grateful Skipper.'

RAY LINDWALL

(Australia)

Growing up in the late 1920s and early 1930s, Ray Lindwall wanted to bowl like Harold Larwood, the Englishman he had watched in the Bodyline series. Later generations would wish to model themselves on Lindwall. 'Imitating Ray Lindwall gave exquisite pleasure, like arrowing through surf or ice-skating,' wrote David Frith in *The Fast Men*. Frith had also played for the St George club in Sydney, which boasts Don Bradman, Lindwall and the leg-spinner Bill 'Tiger' O'Reilly among its alumni. It was O'Reilly who mentored Lindwall at St George.

With a low arm and slingy action, Lindwall was both fast and skilful. He formed a devastating opening partnership with the debonair Keith Miller, with whom he played fifty-one of his sixty-one Tests. The pair emerged in the first Ashes series after the war, in 1946–47, when Lindwall took eighteen wickets in four Tests, including seven for sixty-three in the final Test at Sydney. England, still trying to regroup after the war, were ill-equipped to deal with the ferocity of Lindwall. In the third Test of that series Lindwall also showed he could bat, making a century off eighty-nine balls batting at number nine. At the time it was the second fastest by an Australian.

Lindwall was a significant member of Australia's 1948 Invincibles who routed England 4-0 and left a legacy of admiration and awe. In the second Test at Lord's, when Miller was unable to bowl, Lindwall carried the attack, taking eight wickets in the match, many through sheer pace.

FRED TRUEMAN

(England)

Fred Trueman was magnetic and magnificent, a fast bowler with skill and style but also a compelling ability to hold a crowd to attention, something he later translated into his lengthy career as a radio pundit. A Yorkshireman who combined acerbic wit with blunt speaking, Trueman enjoyed telling batsmen their deficiencies and how he might best exploit them. He was built for fast bowling, strong in the shoulders and hefty in the behind. His unmistakeable mop of jet-black hair trailed in the wind as he charged to the wicket before unleashing fast out-swing with the perfect side-on action. He once joked that the title of his autobiography should be *T'Greatest Fast Bowler Who Ever Drew Breath*.

In the second innings of his Test debut in 1952 on his home ground at Leeds, Trueman reduced India to none for four, taking three wickets in fourteen balls. In his third match at Manchester, he took eight for thirty-one, the best Test figures by a fast bowler at the time. In the second half of the 1950s he formed a lethal opening partnership with Brian Statham, a relentlessly accurate craftsman from Lancashire. In 1964 Trueman became the first man from any country to take 300 Test wickets and finished his career a few Tests later on 307. He could have played more for England but he was forever falling foul of the authorities who mistrusted his earthy views and attitudes, viewing him as something as a liability, particularly on overseas tours.

FRANK TYSON

(England)

In his own words, Frank Tyson was 'a bowler of sensation, who bowled well and fast when he felt right'. Sensation indeed. Comparing the speed of pace bowlers through the ages is impossible and ultimately futile but it is unlikely that any man has bowled faster than 'Typhoon' Tyson did in the remarkable Ashes series of 1954–55. His performance turned the series in England's favour after they had suffered a heavy defeat in the first Test at Brisbane. But before his heroics in the second Test at Sydney came the alarm of being hit on the back of the head by a Ray Lindwall bouncer. Tyson was knocked out but recovered to resume his innings and then destroy Australia on the final day with six wickets. They required only 223 to win but had no answer to Tyson, and his foil Brian Statham, and lost by thirty-eight runs. In the next Test at Melbourne, Australia were seventy-five for two at stumps on day four, chasing 240 on a worn pitch. The following morning, though, they lost their last eight wickets for thirty-six runs in seventy-nine minutes. Tyson, who took seven for twenty-seven, 'blazed through them like a bush fire', according to *Wisden*. He took twenty-eight wickets at twenty apiece in the series, one of England's finest overseas triumphs, but he played only eleven more Tests. He was a thoughtful, intelligent man who became a teacher and commentator after settling in Australia.

Column 15

	86 WI **Hl** Hall
	87 A **Li** Lillee
79 A **Or** O'Reilly	88 WI **Ro** Roberts
80 A **W** Warne	89 WI **Ho** Holding
81 A **Sp** Spofforth	90 WI **Mh** Marshall
82 E **Lw** Larwood	91 WI **Ab** Ambrose
83 A **Ln** Lindwall	92 P **Wa** Akram
84 E **Tm** Trueman	93 SA **Dn** Donald
85 E **Ty** Tyson	94 SA **St** Steyn

WES HALL

(West Indies)

'When I first laid eyes on Wes Hall he was in the next parish,' wrote the broadcaster Tony Cozier of his fellow Barbadian. 'As I scratched my guard the bowler in the far distance at the end of a run that would become as identifiable as any in the game was the latest West Indies tearaway.' Some tearaway. Hall was not the first West Indies fast bowler but it was his partnership in the 1960s with the controversial and equally hostile Charlie Griffith that left a legacy for the many other Caribbean quicks in the decades to come. Hall was tall and muscular with a long run-up; Griffith was less orthodox and was often suspected of 'throwing' his faster delivery.

As well his pace, around 145 kph, Hall was renowned for his stamina. In the tied Test at Brisbane in 1960, he took nine wickets, hauling West Indies back into the match at the end after it seemed that Australia's tail-enders were taking them over the line. After that seminal series, the Australian commentator Johnny Moyes assessed Hall as 'a rare box-office attraction, a man who caught and held the affections of the paying public'. Fearsome, yes, but also immensely popular. At Lord's in 1963, in another epically dramatic Test, he broke the left arm of England batsman Colin Cowdrey. On the final day he bowled unchanged for more than three hours – the entirety of a weather-shortened day – as England ended up six runs short of victory with one wicket remaining. In retirement, Hall became an ordained minister and a Member of Parliament in Barbados.

DENNIS LILLEE

(Australia)

Arms and thighs pumping, dark hair flowing, gold chain swaying and moustache twitching, Dennis Lillee was one of the instruments of Australian success in the mid 1970s.

A beautifully smooth run-up and his leaping, athletic delivery stride were allied to ferocious aggression. His partnership with the unconventional Jeff Thomson demolished England and West Indies in successive series in 1974–75 and 1975–76. What is especially remarkable about those victories is Lillee had already had to fight back from a serious back injury.

Lillee began his Test career as a tearaway fast bowler towards the end of the 1970–71 Ashes. Australia ultimately lost the series, but Lillee made an immediate impact with five wickets at Adelaide. The following year, he came to England, firstly in the Lancashire League where he would learn about English conditions, and then into the Ashes. He took thirty-one wickets, then an Australian record in England, to confirm his special talent. In 1981 he overtook Richie Benaud as Australia's leading Test wicket-taker and later in the year became the greatest wicket-taker of all, beating West Indian Lance Gibbs's haul of 309.

He was a controversial figure too. He once tried to use an aluminium bat – the laws of the game state they must be made of wood – in a Test against England. On the 1981 Ashes tour of England, he and wicket-keeper Rodney Marsh placed a bet on Australia to lose the Headingley when the odds stood at 500-1. England famously won the Test from an almost impossible position. And at Perth once, he kicked out at Javed Miandad after losing his temper at the Pakistan batsman.

ANDY ROBERTS

(West Indies)

Andy Roberts was 'deadpan and deadly', according to Mike Selvey, the former England bowler and one-time opponent of the great Antiguan quick. In *Fire in Babylon*, the story of West Indies' rise, the author Simon Lister wrote: 'His silence could perturb those who didn't know him.' Roberts, who first played Test cricket in 1974, was the godfather of the Caribbean pace phenomenon, a seemingly endless production line of fast bowlers who were integral to their team's domination of international cricket for almost two decades. 'I don't have to sledge. My eyes and the ball do all the sledging for me,' said Roberts himself.

From an early age, he showed that he had intelligence to go with the raw power and pace. Having played a single Test match, he arrived at Hampshire in 1974 as their overseas player and took 119 wickets at an average of only thirteen. 'He is a very shrewd person, someone who knows what he can do and what he can't,' said the Hampshire captain Richard Gilliat. Roberts's enduring party trick – if that isn't to trivialise both the skill and the purpose – was the ability to bowl two bouncers of varying speeds with no discernible change in his action or delivery.

One particular example had unpleasant consequences. At Sydney in 1977, the first season of Kerry Packer's breakaway World Series Cricket, the young Australian left-hander David Hookes was enjoying himself taking on the West Indian quicks, including Michael Holding, Joel Garner and Roberts. Roberts bowled his 'slower' bouncer first to Hookes who took it on. When another one came next ball, Hookes, who was on eighty-one, tried to hit it again but this time was hit in the jaw, an injury that necessitated two days in hospital.

He took only two years and 138 days to reach 100 Test wickets, a record at the time. Although he played Test cricket until 1984, he was at his most devastating in the early part of his career.

MICHAEL HOLDING

(West Indies)

Utilising his childhood talents as a long-jumper and hurdler, West Indies' Michael Holding had the smoothest, most elegant run-up of any fast bowler in history. But the aesthetics would generally be lost on the batsman at the other end, having to face a 145 kph delivery from the man who became known as 'Whispering Death'.

A single, famous over to England's Geoff Boycott at the Kensington Oval in Barbados in 1981 encapsulated his speed and skill. Boycott fended off the first ball, missed the next three, defended another short one and then saw his off stump disappear out of the turf from the final ball. 'Bridgetown exploded,' wrote Scyld Berry in *The Observer*. 'They had come over the walls and through the fences, they had sat on the stand roofs with such an expectation in mind.'

Holding's barrage of short stuff against England's balding veteran Brian Close at Manchester in 1976 was another frighteningly compelling passage of express bowling. In the final match of that series, Holding produced one of the greatest performances by a bowler of his type. On a slow, dry pitch in a match containing two double centuries and 1,507 runs, Holding took fourteen wickets, twelve of them bowled or lbw. He was too fast. In all he took 249 wickets in sixty Tests between 1975 and 1987, leaving him sixth in West Indies' all-time list. His measured, laconic punditry, articulated in his rich, deep Jamaican voice, has made him an immensely popular television commentator around the world.

MALCOLM MARSHALL

(West Indies)

West Indies had bigger, quicker and nastier quicks than Malcolm Marshall but few, if any, were better and none possessed quite such a complete package of skills. He was also a very useful lower-order batsman.

Neither tall nor well-built, Marshall had an exceptional work ethic that allowed him to bowl long and often and with an array of weapons at his disposal. He had a sprinter's approach to the wicket and his pace came from his whippy arm speed. His out-swinger was vicious and his bouncer, because it was perhaps less expected than from some of his peers, was skiddy and awkward.

Marshall had the unenviable task of replacing Andy Roberts as Hampshire's overseas player in 1979 but he filled those shoes and then some. In the summer of 1982 he took 134 wickets, the most in an English season since 1967 and a figure that has not been close to being broken since. For the West Indies, many of Marshall's highlights were against England and none more than the remarkable Test at Leeds on the 1984 'blackwash' tour when the home side were defeated in all five Tests. Marshall had broken his left thumb in the field on the first day, but came out to bat one-handed at number eleven to help Larry Gomes reach a century. Then, with his left arm in a cast, he took seven wickets, varying his pace astutely to benefit from the bowler-friendly conditions.

Marshall went on to take twenty-four wickets at eighteen runs each in the series. Four years later in England he was even more devastating, taking thirty-five at twelve. His nous and range of skills made him equally potent overseas, as he showed with thirty-three wickets in six Tests in India in 1983–84.

CURTLY AMBROSE

(West Indies)

Everyone looked up to Curtly Ambrose – literally. He used his height (two metres) to great effect and showed why his decision not to pursue a basketball career in the United States was very much cricket's, and specifically West Indies', gain. When he took a wicket (405 in Tests and 225 in ODIs), he would be a visible totem among his shorter teammates as earnest, unsmiling high-fives would be exchanged. Meanwhile, at her home in Swetes Village, Antigua, Curtly's mum Hillie would run out of the house and ring a bell to acknowledge the achievement. The great West Indies fast bowlers were not generally given to verbal jousts with batsmen, preferring to let their potent bowling do the talking. Ambrose took this silent treatment off the field as well, rebuffing interview requests with: 'Curtly talk to no man.'

He had a rhythmic and springy, but economical, approach to the wicket. The right wrist would cock like a trigger then fire the ball down. His height and the wrist snap allowed Ambrose to make the lift off a good length. When he got on a roll he was unstoppable. At Perth in 1993, Australia were doing fine at eighty-five for two on the first day until Ambrose produced one of his most devastating spells: seven wickets for one run in thirty-two balls to reduce the home side to 119 all out. They never recovered and West Indies won by an innings.

In Trinidad a year later, England were beginning their second innings on the fourth evening with victory in mind. They needed 194 to win and claw their way into the series. By the close of play, they were forty for eight. Their captain, Mike Atherton, went lbw to the first ball of the innings, fear and panic spreading like a virus through their dressing room. Ambrose took six for twenty-four, and eleven in the match as England were dismissed for forty-six, only a single run more than their lowest ever Test score.

WASIM AKRAM

(Pakistan)

Simply the most prolific (414 Test wickets, 502 in ODIs) and, by most judgements, the best left-arm pace bowler of all time. Wasim Akram's partnership with right-armer Waqar Younis was devastatingly destructive and uncannily complementary. The pair are two of the top five Test wicket-takers through the 1990s and as a double act they lie fourth in the Test all-time list, having taken 555 wickets in 107 innings in which they bowled together. They are fourth on the ODI list with 581.

Both were seriously fast. Wasim had the more classical, economical action with a high delivery leap and whippy arm speed. He could swing it both ways too.

Waqar's angle of delivery was low, at times almost round-arm. He was one of the best bowlers with an old ball – balls are required to last eighty overs in a Test innings – and could produce unplayable, late swing, known as 'reverse' swing because it would move in the opposite direction to the expected direction of a newer ball.

In 1984 Wasim was at a Pakistan Under-19 camp in Rawalpindi while a Pakistan board Patron's XI, captained by the great Javed Miandad, were preparing for a match against the touring New Zealanders. Wasim got to bowl at Miandad who was so impressed that he insisted that the teenager be picked for their game. Having taken seven for fifty in New Zealand's first innings it's fair to say that he made a decent impression.

He took wickets all over the world and only in South Africa, where he played only two Tests, did he average more than thirty with the ball. Only two bowlers have taken more wickets in World Cups than Wasim and he was man of the match in the 1992 final, his two wickets in two balls shifting the game against England in Pakistan's favour. He was also a free-hitting left-handed batsman with a Test best of 257 not out, which included twelve sixes, against Zimbabwe.

ALLAN DONALD

(South Africa)

In a golden era for pace bowling dominated by West Indians and Pakistanis, Allan Donald was, as his nickname of 'White Lightning' suggests, the fastest white man around. He was the spearhead of South Africa's bowling attack for the first decade of their post-apartheid readmission into official international cricket.

A man of gentle and polite charm off the field, he was a fierce competitor on it, never better exemplified than during his epic duel with England opening batsman Mike Atherton at Nottingham in 1998. 'Two giants of the modern game fought a titanic battle,' reported *Wisden*.

England were chasing 247 to win and level the five-Test series with one match to play. Donald's first spell was pushing 145 kph and then, with England nicely placed on eighty-two for one, he returned. He peppered Atherton and when the batsman gloved one to the keeper Donald assumed he'd got his man. Atherton was given not out and Donald fumed. The next ball was edged to the boundary. 'The bowler snarled at Atherton,' *Wisden* said, 'who stared impassively back.' When Atherton's partner, Nasser Hussain, was dropped by keeper Mark Boucher, Donald raised his face to the heavens and let out a primeval roar. After the match, which England won, both Donald and Atherton were sharing a beer in the dressing room.

He took twelve wickets to bowl to South Africa to victory over India at Port Elizabeth in 1992, their first Test win since readmission and the country's first since 1970. Other highlights included Johannesburg in 1999 when he and Shaun Pollock, his new-ball partner for a chunk of his career, took nineteen of twenty England wickets in helpful conditions. He was the first South African bowler to take 300 Test wickets.

94	SA
St	
Steyn	

DALE STEYN

(South Africa)

First came the pace and then came the control. Putting the two together is a fearsome combination. At 1.79 m, Dale Steyn is not a bang-it-in fast bowler. His modus operandi is to swing the ball viciously and late at around 145 kph, bowling which is too good for most batsmen. The slightly skiddy trajectory adds another level of difficulty for the man at the other end. Add in a mean, pursed-lip stare and you have the ultimate twenty-first-century speed merchant. In 2008 he became the fastest South African bowler to reach 100 Test wickets and in 2015 he became the fastest from any country, in terms of balls bowled, to reach 400 Test wickets.

Another remarkable strand of Steyn's success is his record in Asia – so often a graveyard for pace bowlers, especially those without regular experience of the slower pitches. Yet among bowlers who have taken fifty or more wickets in Asia, Steyn averages a Test wicket every six-and-a-half overs, a strike-rate that is second only to the great Pakistani Waqar Younis. At Ahmedabad in 2008, on a surprisingly grassy – and thus bowler-friendly – pitch, Steyn sent India packing in only twenty overs for seventy-six, their second lowest Test total at home.

Later that year at Melbourne he had the sort of ludicrously stellar match beyond even the most extravagant of dreams. South Africa had never won a Test series in Australia but they were one-nil up in a three-match rubber after an improbable run chase at Perth. In the second Test they were tottering at 251 for eight, still 143 behind Australia's first innings, when Steyn came in to bat with J. P. Duminy. Steyn had already taken five wickets in the first innings but batting is not his strong suit, hence his lowly position in the order. Almost four hours later Steyn was out for seventy-six after a partnership of 180 with Duminy, the third highest for the ninth wicket in history. The once mighty Australians were on their knees by now and Steyn humbled them again in the second innings, taking five more wickets. South Africa won the Test by nine wickets and had an unassailable, historic 2-0 lead.

Innovators
& Pioneers

Some players in this chapter are greats of the game; others have simply made such a significant impact that they deserve inclusion. Cricket's technical complexity means that its elite participants have forever been searching for ways to gain a competitive advantage. The balance between bat and ball is the game's delicate ecosystem and whenever one appears to hold sway, there will be genius at work in some corner of the globe to counteract.

The political, racial and social landscape of cricket has been a fundamental part of the sport's history. The game has been slow to grow beyond its traditional post-colonial territories but in those countries and regions it is woven into the fabric of society. Cricket has always carried resonance way beyond the boundaries of the field on which it is played and some of the individuals in this chapter have been instrumental in changing perceptions, attitudes and realities.

W. G. GRACE

(England)

In 2015, a century after his death, there were two new books about William Gilbert Grace. The world, let alone cricket, is a vastly different place to the one that he inhabited and yet his shadow still looms large. It is hard to think of another sport where a man who operated well over a hundred years ago is still synonymous with the game. W. G. – his initials will do. And then there's the beard, decades ahead of the hipster curve.

Grace popularised cricket and bestrode the sport for more than forty years. He started when he was sixteen and was still playing into his fifties. He scored more than 50,000 first-class runs and his batting average is more than twice his bowling average – a sign of true class in an all-rounder. Many of his innings were played on terrible pitches that would seem alien to the modern game. He passed 1,000 runs in a season twenty-eight times. In 1895, aged forty-six, he scored 1,000 runs in the month of May alone, a feat achieved only twice since, and made his hundredth hundred. He also took 100 or more wickets in a season ten times.

The numbers, though, do little justice to the man. His batting was unconventional, full of attacking, aggressive intent, contrary to the orthodoxy of the time. 'It helps to think of him, just a little, as one of the great Victorian inventors,' wrote Richard Tomlinson, his latest biographer. He made 152 on his Test debut at The Oval in 1889 and captained England in thirteen of his twenty-two Tests, winning eight of them. Also a doctor in Bristol, Grace played as an amateur though there were regular disputes and controversies regarding remuneration for 'expenses'. He was famously competitive and the stories of his gamesmanship are legion.

KUMAR SHRI RANJITSINHJI

(England)

Ranji was the game's first great non-white cricketer, a unique talent and a remarkable character. He was an Indian prince who played for Cambridge University (where he was known as 'Smith'), Sussex and England. According to Sydney Southerton, one-time editor of *Wisden*, Ranji 'was to become and to remain from 1895 until 1912 … the most talked-of man in cricket'. He was a batsman of flair and innovation who is credited with developing strokes such as the late cut (behind square on the off side) and the leg glance, which are standard tools of any modern batsman. 'He seldom played a genuine forward stroke,' wrote Simon Wilde in his biography, *Ranji: A Genius Rich and Strange*.

Ranji scored 62 and 154 not out on his Test debut against Australia at Manchester in 1896, though he played only fifteen Tests in all. His first-class record was exceptional: almost 25,000 runs at an average of 56, one of the highest in history. He passed 3,000 runs in the 1899 and 1900 seasons, scoring a record five double centuries in the latter.

His contemporary Gilbert Jessop wrote of him: 'From the moment he stepped out of the pavilion he drew all eyes and held them. No one who saw him bat will ever forget it. He was the first man I ever knew who wore silk shirts, and there was something almost romantic about the very flow of his sleeves and the curves of his shoulders.' As a man, he was charming, rakish and slippery as many of his creditors found to their cost.

TILLAKARATNE DILSHAN

(Sri Lanka)

It was in 2009, while preparing for the Twenty20 Indian Premier League, that Sri Lankan Tillakaratne Dilshan first attempted the shot that would soon bear his name. He tried to play a sweep shot against a quickish delivery from a bowling machine and managed to flick the ball over his head. '"Wow, this is something," I thought to myself, and tried to play it again,' he said. He then played the shot for real in an IPL match for Delhi Daredevils against Deccan Chargers, twice scooping Australian seamer Ryan Harris over his own and the wicket-keeper's head. The 'Dilscoop' was born, and has since been copied and adapted by batsmen all over the world. It is now almost a standard limited-overs shot.

'He is someone who needs to be kept on the edge,' said Paul Farbrace, Sri Lanka's former assistant coach. And certainly Dilshan's slightly piratical look, with earrings, gold chains and goatee beard, always suggested someone willing to push the boundaries. He took his invention into the World Twenty20 in 2009 in England, helping Sri Lanka to the final and himself to the player of the tournament award. Having made two fifties in the first two games of the tournament, he scored an unbeaten ninety-six in the semi-final against West Indies and was within a single shot of emulating one of his opponents that day, Chris Gayle, in becoming only the second man to score a T20 international hundred. In 2015 he became the eleventh man, and the fourth Sri Lankan, to pass 10,000 one-day international runs.

GEORGE HEADLEY

(West Indies)

In England and Australia, George Headley was known as the 'black Bradman'. In the Caribbean Don Bradman was referred to as the 'white Headley'. He was born in Panama, where his father worked on building the canal, but moved to Jamaica at the age of ten. There this small, compact right-hander emerged as the first great West Indies batsman. 'At every level of the game, in fact, he scored an avalanche of runs with a style and brilliance few of any age have matched,' said *Wisden* in his obituary.

Headley's career, like so many others, was interrupted by the Second World War but his twenty-two Tests for West Indies between 1930 and 1954 yielded enough evidence to confirm his brilliance. His Test career average of 60.83 is bettered only by the South African Graeme Pollock (by fractions) and, of course, Bradman. In his debut Test series, in 1930 against England, he scored four centuries (only one man has ever scored more in a series) and a total of 703 runs in the four Tests. In the third match in Guyana, a century in each innings helped the West Indies to their maiden Test victory. When England returned to the Caribbean four years later, he scored 485 runs in the four Tests, more than 200 more than the next best on either side, as West Indies won their first Test series. His son Ron played two Tests for West Indies in 1973 and his grandson Dean played Tests and one-dayers for England in the 1990s.

99   SL
Rn
Ranatunga

ARJUNA RANATUNGA

(Sri Lanka)

Stout and combative, Arjuna Ranatunga's leadership helped transform Sri Lanka from charming amateurs into a credible Test-playing nation and, in 1996, one-day World Cup winners.

He played, as an eighteen-year-old left-hander, in Sri Lanka's inaugural Test match against England in Colombo in 1982 and scored a fifty on day one that helped his side recover after a bad start. He became captain in 1989 and in 1995 led Sri Lanka to their first Test win overseas, against New Zealand at Napier.

Later that year, in the Boxing Day Test at Melbourne, came the first great challenge of his captaincy when spinner Muttiah Muralitharan was no-balled for throwing by umpire Darrell Hair and in a subsequent match by Ross Emerson, standing in his first international. Just over three years later, Emerson called Murali again in a one-day international against England at Adelaide. 'Pandemonium broke out,' according to *Wisden*. An incensed Ranatunga led his players to the boundary where he conducted discussions with Sri Lankan officials before the match resumed. Ranatunga was charged by the ICC, cricket's global governing body, with various offences but got away with a suspended six-match ban. Umpire Emerson, who it emerged was actually signed off with stress from his day job, was stood down for the rest of the series.

The greatest day in Ranatunga's career, and indeed Sri Lankan cricket history, was 17 March 1996. The first Asian World Cup, which Sri Lanka co-hosted with India and Pakistan, faced many logistical troubles, including the refusal of Australia and West Indies to play in Sri Lanka following a bomb blast in Colombo. Against the odds, Sri Lanka reached the final by defeating India at Kolkata. Well on top, they were awarded the match by default after the crowd rioted. Then in the final at Lahore, Sri Lanka upset the favourites Australia. After smothering the Aussie batsmen with spin, Sri Lanka made light of their target of 242. Aravinda de Silva made a century and Ranatunga was there at the end after a brisk, unbeaten forty-seven.

LEARIE CONSTANTINE

(West Indies)

Learie Constantine was both an entertainer and by extension an aggressor, but as the first great – and famous – West Indies cricketer, he also has pioneering, mould-breaking status. According to the author C. L. R. James, Constantine rebelled 'against the revolting contrast between his first-class status as a cricketer and a third-class status as a man'. The grandson of a slave, he toured England with West Indies in 1923 and 1928 and on the latter trip was hired by Nelson Cricket Club in the Lancashire League as a professional player. He played there with great success until the start of the Second World War, attracting crowds of up to 14,000. In the decades to come countless players from the Caribbean would become stars of league – and indeed county – cricket around England and Wales.

Constantine was a muscular and attacking batsman, a bowler capable of considerable pace and a brilliantly athletic fielder, particularly in the covers. One match on the 1928 tour, for West Indies against Middlesex at Lord's, stands out. In the West Indies' first innings, Constantine made 86 out of 230 when no other batsman made more than 30. West Indies were 150 behind after the first innings but Constantine took 7 for 57, including one spell of 6 for 11, to reduce Middlesex to 136 all out and leave West Indies 259 to win. At 121 for 5, the victory looked gone but in came Constantine and made 103 out of the 133 scored while he was at the crease. West Indies won by three wickets and, said *Wisden*, 'Lord's erupted: and next day all cricketing England accepted a new major figure.'

After retiring from cricket, Constantine worked in the British Ministry of Labour, was High Commissioner for Trinidad and Tobago in the 1960s, knighted in 1962 and became a life peer in the UK Parliament's House of Lords in 1969.

FRANK WORRELL

(West Indies)

'He was only at the beginning,' wrote Sir Learie Constantine after the untimely death of Frank Worrell, the first appointed black captain of West Indies, from leukaemia in 1967, aged only forty-two. 'Had he lived he would surely have become a statesman in world affairs,' wrote Christopher Martin-Jenkins. Worrell, one of the legendary 'Three Ws' from Barbados – the others being Clyde Walcott and Everton Weekes – was a man of true substance who had a profound effect on the Caribbean region and cricket around the world. 'A man of strong convictions, a brave man, and it goes without saying, a great cricketer,' added Constantine.

Lithe and stylish, Worrell made his debut for West Indies at twenty-three in 1948 against England, scoring ninety-seven and 131 in two of his first three innings. But it was in England two years later that he and the West Indies truly established themselves as forces to be reckoned with. Following the famous Lord's Test when the spinners Sonny Ramadhin and Alf Valentine caused havoc, Worrell made hay in the third match at Trent Bridge. He put on 241 with Weekes and made 261 himself in only five-and-a-half hours, as West Indies won by ten wickets. He made a century in the final match at The Oval, which the West Indies also won to complete their first series victory in England.

Eventually, by the end of the 1950s, the West Indies board deemed it acceptable for a black man to captain its cricket team. Worrell was that man and his first undertaking proved to be his lasting legacy. The 1950s had been a dull time for cricket globally. Safety-first, attritional tactics were sucking the life out of the game. In the 1960–61 series against Australia, Worrell's West Indians changed the game. Playing with zest and zeal, they made a nation of friends. Their series kicked off with the astonishing Brisbane Test, the first tie in history, and ended, after a 2-1 defeat, with West Indies receiving a tickertape parade through Melbourne before their departure. 'A send-off the like of which is normally reserved for royalty and national heroes,' said *Wisden*.

102	E
DI	
D'Oliveira	

BASIL D'OLIVEIRA

(England)

Basil D'Oliveira was the catalyst for South Africa's twenty-two-year isolation from international cricket. He had been a talented all-rounder in his native South Africa but because of his skin colour – he was designated a Cape Coloured – he was barred from participating in mainstream white competition.

With the support of, among others, the journalist and broadcaster, John Arlott, D'Oliveira emigrated to the UK in 1960. At first he played successfully for Middleton in the Central Lancashire League, then joined Worcestershire in 1965 and made his England debut in 1966 when he was already thirty-four. He was a powerful, attacking batsman and useful medium-paced swing bowler. After two years in the England side, he was dropped after one Test of the 1968 Ashes series only to return for the final match at The Oval as a late replacement due to illness. 'Dolly' took his chance, made 158 and was presumed to be a likely selection for the winter tour to South Africa.

The selectors overlooked him, causing widespread public consternation and suspicions that the South African government was leaning on MCC, who ran English cricket. Following the withdrawal of Tom Cartwright through injury, D'Oliveira was picked but the South African Prime Minister, John Vorster, announced in Parliament that the player's inclusion was unacceptable. England's tour was cancelled and South Africa did not play an official international again until 1991. D'Oliveira continued to play for England until 1972. Since 2004 England's Test series against South Africa have been played for the Basil D'Oliveira Trophy.

MICHAEL BEVAN

(Australia)

There was a time when the term 'finisher' was the exclusive preserve of the footballing goal-scorer. And then at some point in the 1990s, it passed into common usage to describe a batsman who was particularly adept at closing out a limited-overs innings, shepherding his team to victory under extreme pressure. The original and the best was the Australian left-hander Michael Bevan.

Muscular and intense, Bevan hailed, unusually for Australian international cricketers, from the nation's administrative capital, Canberra, though he played most of his state cricket for the powerhouse of New South Wales. He made his international debut in 1994 and his eureka moment came at Sydney on New Year's Day, 1996, when he hit the last ball of a one-day international against West Indies for four, immediately receiving a high-five from the bowler Roger Harper. Australia had been 38 for 6, chasing 173, and they won by a single wicket thanks to Bevan's 78 not out. 'It seems this one night will always be my signature piece,' the batsman wrote in *The Best of Bevan*, with more than a tinge of regret.

Bevan was such a good one-day batsman that his quest for Test-match recognition – still the ultimate affirmation – was left unfulfilled even though he did play eighteen times. He performed a similar feat of escapology at Port Elizabeth in the 2003 World Cup to break England hearts and help Australia on the way to the second of two World Cup titles they would win in Bevan's career. His calm temperament and geometric ability to place the ball into areas unguarded by fielders left him with the phenomenal ODI batting average of fifty-three.

104   SA

BI

Bland

COLIN BLAND

(South Africa)

'Bland is the man who transformed fielding from an obligation to an art,' wrote Glenn Moore in the *Independent* in a 2011 interview. Colin Bland, Rhodesia-born but a South African Test player, was decades ahead of his time in practising and perfecting his fielding ability. At his peak in the mid 1960s, he begat the likes of his countryman Jonty Rhodes who took ground-fielding to new heights in the 1990s. These days, with run-saving so precious in high-octane, high-scoring limited-overs matches, brilliant fielding is a prerequisite for successful teams. But in Bland's time, as Moore alluded, fielding was very much the poor relation of cricket's tripartite family of skills. He was, it should be noted, an attacking middle-order batsman who averaged forty-nine in his twenty-one Tests and indeed, at The Oval in 1965, scored the last century in South Africa–England Tests for twenty-nine years.

Two moments from earlier in that tour define Bland's brilliance. In the first Test at Lord's, England were going well on 240 for 4, trailing South Africa's first-innings score by only 40, and with Ken Barrington nine away from a century. Barrington pushed the ball into the leg side and set off for a run. Bland sprinted from his position at mid-on, picked up the ball, turned and threw down the stumps at the bowler's end in one fluid movement to dismiss Barrington. He later also ran out the England keeper, Jim Parks. England were pegged back, the match was drawn (after a thrilling finish) and South Africa went on to win the series.

Just after the Lord's Test, the South Africans were playing Kent at Canterbury. 'We were late starting because of drizzle and Colin Cowdrey [Kent captain] asked me if I would do a little show,' recalled Bland. 'I was on a hiding to nothing because it was wet but they spoilt me by giving me three stumps – I always practised with one.' Bland hit the stumps twelve times out of fifteen.

MOHAMMAD NABI

(Afghanistan)

The emergence of the Afghanistan national team over the past fifteen years is one of cricket's greatest success stories and Mohammad Nabi, who captained them in their inaugural World Cup appearance in 2015, is their standard bearer. In common with many of his compatriots, Nabi lived in a refugee camp in Pakistan after his parents had fled the war in Afghanistan between the Soviet Union and the Mujahideen in 1985. He developed a love of cricket in Pakistan and took that passion back to Afghanistan.

A turning point for Nabi, and Afghanistan cricket, was a match in 2006 against a touring side from Marylebone Cricket Club (MCC, who own Lord's), led by Mike Gatting, the former England captain. Afghanistan thrashed the MCC side by 171 runs and Nabi, a super-attacking batsman and off-spin bowler, smashed 116. He and his teammate Hameed Hassan, a fast bowler, were invited to join MCC's academy of young cricketers based at Lord's.

The first big breakthrough for Afghanistan came with their qualification for the 2010 World Twenty20, a watershed moment that was captured in the documentary film *Out of the Ashes,* and was even mentioned in dispatches by Hillary Clinton, the then US Secretary of State. During the qualification tournament for the 2015 fifty-over World Cup, Nabi's father was kidnapped and remained missing for two months. He was found while Nabi was on the way to Namibia for a qualifier. 'Nabi celebrated by playing the match of his life,' wrote Tim Wigmore in *Second XI: Cricket in its Outposts*. 'He smashed eighty-one not out from forty-five balls, showing the audacity, clean timing and effortless power evident when he played for MCC Young Cricketers seven years earlier. He then made sure of victory by taking 5-12 with his crafty off spin.' Nabi also made the winning hit against Kenya to secure World

Cup qualification. At the tournament itself in Australia and New Zealand, they notched their first win, beating Scotland in a nail-biting one-wicket victory.

106	E
Hf	
Heyhoe Flint	

RACHAEL HEYHOE FLINT

(England)

Rachael Heyhoe Flint has been central to the development, promotion and mainstream acceptance of women's cricket for more than forty years. She was one of the instigators and then the winning captain for England of the inaugural women's World Cup in 1973 – two years before the men's version appeared. Again as England captain, she was one of the first women to play at Lord's – against Australia in 1976 – after many years of campaigning.

Heyhoe Flint also campaigned hard for Marylebone Cricket Club (the private club which owns Lord's) to allow women to become members. After a nine-year battle even to get the club to hold a vote, the members finally allowed women in 1998. She was among the first female members of MCC, the first woman to be inducted into the International Cricket Council hall of fame and in 2010 was one of the first two women appointed to the management board of the England and Wales Cricket Board (ECB).

She took great pleasure at the announcement in 2014 that eighteen England women cricketers would be awarded professional contracts by the ECB. 'That's absolutely amazing,' she told the *Observer*, 'it really brings life full circle back to the time when I would walk round the crowds collecting coppers, silver and pound coins to raise money for the team, and then drive home with it sitting in the footwell of my car. It's wonderful that those women are regarded almost on parity with the opportunities offered to men.'

ANDY FLOWER

(Zimbabwe)

Andy Flower was a highly accomplished left-handed batsman and wicket-keeper, and Zimbabwe's best batsman by some distance. He was also a thoughtful, sometimes intense, successful coach of England from 2009 to 2013.

But his mark on cricket history was made in Harare on 10 February 2003, when he and teammate Henry Olonga, the first black man to play for Zimbabwe, made a political protest during their home World Cup against the oppressive regime of Robert Mugabe. The two players took the field for their first match of the tournament against Namibia wearing black armbands and issued the following statement: 'In doing so we are mourning the death of democracy in our beloved Zimbabwe. In doing so we are making a silent plea to those responsible to stop the abuse of human rights in Zimbabwe. In doing so, we pray that our small action may help to restore sanity and dignity to our nation.'

At the time of writing, Mugabe is still the president of Zimbabwe. Flower and Olonga, meanwhile, never played for their country again after the 2003 World Cup. Both went to the UK: Flower to resume his county career with Essex and then take up coaching: Olonga, a classically trained singer, has a career as a musician and after-dinner speaker.

MAHENDRA SINGH DHONI

(India)

Almost everything about M. S. Dhoni has defied convention. From the small-town upbringing, the shoulder-length locks and the flat-footed but ferocious batsmanship, Dhoni carved a unique niche in Indian and global cricket.

As captain of India, he hit a six to win the World Cup on home soil; he raised eyebrows in a Lord's Test match by removing his wicket-keeping pads to bowl medium-pace and almost having Kevin Pietersen lbw; in the same series he recalled England batsman Ian Bell to the crease after he considered a run out to be contrary to the spirit of the game. There is his obsession with motorbikes – he owns more than a dozen and in 2012 he even set up a professional racing bikes team. And then there is his love for all things military – he is an honorary Lieutenant Colonel in the Parachute Regiment. In 2015, *Forbes* magazine ranked him as the twenty-third wealthiest athlete in the world, estimating his earnings at $31 million, $27 million of which comes from sponsorship deals and endorsements.

Emerging from the mining state of Jharkhand in eastern India, he first played for India in 2004 and in only his fifth one-day international smashed 148 not out off 123 balls against Pakistan. He averages more than fifty with the bat in ODIs and scores at a terrific lick. He has the cold-blooded ruthlessness to close games out but also the relish for the spotlight – an irresistible combination. He led his side to victory in the inaugural World Twenty20 tournament in 2007. In the 2011 World Cup final, at Mumbai, Dhoni promoted himself in the batting order ahead of the in-form Yuvraj Singh to take his side home against Sri Lanka. His top score in the tournament had been only thirty-four yet he made ninety-one not out, completing India's win – the first World Cup triumph by a host nation – with a straight six. The following day, he appeared in his team blazer and tie with his head shaved, the luxurious locks gone. From rock star to statesman in one session at the barber's.

BERNARD BOSANQUET

(England)

Bernard Bosanquet invented the googly (or 'Bosie' as it has been known in Australia), the delivery that a wrist-spinner bowls out of the back rather than the front of the hand and spins from off to leg, contrary to the standard leg-break. The best practitioners can deceive a batsman by bowling the googly with no discernible change in their action.

Bosanquet was a tall all-rounder who played for Oxford University, Middlesex and briefly England at the turn of the twentieth century. He claimed the googly was invented around 1897 when he was playing a game with a tennis ball on a table called 'twisti-twosti' where the idea was to bounce the ball on the table in such a way so your opponent could not catch it.

Bosanquet worked out that if you could make a ball spin in the opposite direction to how it appeared then you could deceive your opponent. He began to practise it and when at Oxford became something of a circus act during the lunch interval of matches, required to bowl the googly at the opposition's best batsman. 'If this pitched on the right place it probably hit him on the knee, everyone shrieked with laughter, and I was led away and locked up for the day,' he wrote in *Wisden*.

Bosanquet's best performance for England came at Nottingham in 1905 when he bowled Australia out in the second innings, taking 8 for 107, in a big England victory. Yet he played only two more Test matches. His son Reginald was a television newscaster in the 1970s.

110	A
Bu	
Benaud	

RICHIE BENAUD

(Australia)

To several generations of cricket lovers, Richie Benaud was the voice of summer, a magnificently precise and much-imitated broadcaster who fronted television coverage for the BBC and Channel 4 in the UK and Channel 9 in his native Australia. But he had an illustrious playing career as a dashing, leg-spinning all-rounder and Ashes-winning captain. His attacking instincts brought joy to the early 1960s after a turgid decade. And in the mid 1970s when the entrepreneur Kerry Packer was revolutionising the game with his breakaway World Series Cricket circuit Benaud was the man he turned to as a guiding light and someone who commanded the respect of the world's best players.

Benaud had a slow start to his Test career before bursting into life on a tour of South Africa in 1957–58 when he scored two centuries and took thirty wickets in five Tests. He became captain after that and immediately won the Ashes (he did not lose any of his three series as captain). He played his part in the remarkable 1960–61 home series against Frank Worrell's West Indies that included the first ever tied Test and brought so much enjoyment. The 1961 Ashes in England was 'a personal triumph for Richie Benaud', according to *Wisden,* which praised Australia's 'almost carefree policy throughout their five months' stay'. The fourth Test at Manchester was possibly Benaud's greatest moment. With the series poised at 1-1 and England 150 for one, chasing 256 to win, Benaud came up with a tactical masterstroke. He decided to change his line of attack and bowl his leg-spin around the wicket into the footmarks that had been created by England's pace bowler Fred Trueman. He removed key man Ted Dexter for seventy-six and proceeded to take six for seventy, leading his side to a fifty-four-run victory and retention of the Ashes.

SAQLAIN MUSHTAQ

(Pakistan)

For the right-arm off-spin bowler, the traditional armoury is relatively limited. The stock delivery is spun from the fingers into the right-handed batsman. The variation was essentially a straight delivery. Pakistan's Saqlain Mushtaq pushed the envelope by developing the *doosra* (Urdu for 'the other one') that would still appear to be an off-spinner but in fact turn away from the right-handed batsman. He set the template for a number of international bowlers, mostly from Asia – including India's Harbhajan Singh, Sri Lankan Muttiah Muralitharan and later Pakistani Saeed Ajmal – to have the *doosra* as part of their toolbox as they tried to combat batsmen with ever more powerful bats playing on increasingly docile pitches in the late 1990s. Saqlain says he learned to bowl it first while playing with a table-tennis ball and later with a taped-up tennis ball: the sphere of choice on the streets of urban Pakistan. He reached 100 one-day international wickets in the fewest matches of any bowler but his finest moment came at Chennai in 1998–99, in the first Test between India and Pakistan for nine years. With India needing only seventeen to win with four wickets left, Saqlain took three of them, including that of Sachin Tendulkar who was on 136. Pakistan won by twelve runs.

MUTTIAH MURALITHARAN

(Sri Lanka)

Sri Lanka's greatest bowler and the leading Test wicket-taker of all time was not a rebel by design: he was just a uniquely talented spinner who broke the conventions of the art – and, according to two Australian umpires, the laws of the game.

Murali was a popular teammate and a charming opponent with a smile never far from his cheerful face.

An elbow deformity meant he couldn't fully straighten his right arm so he bowled with a bent one. An exceptionally flexible wrist allowed to him to spin the ball hard into the right-handed batsman, and also, with a chest-on bowling action, to float a delivery that turned away from the batsman – the *doosra*. Suspicion that he was illegally throwing or chucking the ball followed him for most of his career and in the Boxing Day Test at Melbourne in 1995, he was 'called' by Australian umpire Darrell Hair. Hair, who a decade later was at the centre of Pakistan's forfeit of a Test match in England, no-balled Muralitharan seven times in three overs for throwing. Three years later another Australian umpire Ross Emerson did the same in a one-day match.

Murali spent much of his career undergoing scientific tests to prove the legality of his action but amid all the controversy (and, in some quarters, animosity) Murali kept on twirling away and taking wickets by the bucket load. He was a part of Sri Lanka's seminal World Cup win in 1996 and also their run to the final in 2007. In 1998 at The Oval, when Sri Lanka were still given only one Test against England, he stunned the hosts by taking sixteen wickets in a huge victory. He finished his career with precisely 800 Test wickets during a memorable and emotional farewell against India at Galle in 2010. He also took 534 ODI wickets and left the international stage following a third World Cup final appearance, against India in 2011.

Often the only Tamil in the team during years of violent ethnic conflict, Murali was viewed as an unifying ambassador for the country. He invested time and money into the rebuilding of shattered lives following the 2004 tsunami.

MAKHAYA NTINI

(South Africa)

The first black African to play for South Africa, Makhaya Ntini was a tireless fast bowler who was an integral part of his country's pace attack for most of the 2000s. He finished his career with 390 Test wickets and across all international formats has one of the best strike-rates of all time.

Ntini was a goatherd in the Eastern Cape when he was spotted by the South African cricket development programme, searching for black talent to make the national side at least someway representative of the black-majority population. Ntini then went on to further his cricket at the prestigious Dale College. In 1998 at Perth he made his debut in a one-dayer against New Zealand. His reaction when told of his selection was: 'Is this a joke? I don't believe you.' A year later his career hung in the balance when he was convicted of rape. Although he was later acquitted on appeal, he spent two years out of the side.

In 2003 came a marvellously symbolic achievement when he became the first South African bowler to take ten wickets in a match at Lord's. He followed that with twenty-nine wickets in four Tests against West Indies. In the 2005–06 season he was 'workhorse and strike bowler combined', according to *Wisden*, while taking nineteen wickets (almost as many as South Africa's other four bowlers combined) in a tough 3-0 series defeat to Australia. He played his last Test in 2009, retired in 2012 and opened a cricket academy in 2014.

LASITH MALINGA

(Sri Lanka)

In an age of specialist coaches, academies and a general homogenisation of the game, the sight of Lasith Malinga's extraordinary round-arm action flinging down thunderbolts has been a reminder of cricket's glorious individuality. His mop of unruly hair, often partially dyed blond, only added to the cult of the man who became known as Malinga the Slinger.

Malinga credits his unusual action to his learning to bowl with a tennis ball while growing up near Galle. Having made a splash in Sri Lanka's domestic tournament, he toured Australia with the national side in 2004. The following year in New Zealand, he caused such consternation that the home-team batsmen asked the umpires if they would change their dark trousers because the trajectory of Malinga's action was so low they were struggling to see the ball.

He played only thirty Test matches, preferring to concentrate on the shorter forms of the game to preserve a body that was under constant strain because of his unusual action. But his ability to nail the yorker, delivered at fearsome speed towards a batsman's feet, made him the perfect man to close out a one-day or Twenty20 innings. In 2011 he became the first bowler to take three one-day international hat-tricks. The first of those came in the 2007 World Cup in the Caribbean when he took four South African wickets in four balls. Overall in that tournament he took eighteen wickets at an average of only 15.77 runs each to help Sri Lanka to the final.

Index

Acknowledgements

Various friends and colleagues have been vital sounding-boards and sources of wisdom for this project, notably my some-time collaborator Marcus Williams and my Wimbledon Corinthians CC team-mates Brian Clifford and Theo Moore, whose knowledge of the real Periodic Table filled an essential gap in the author's scientific education.